W9-CQY-820

A ROTHMAN FOUNDATION PUBLICATION

שירות ותשבחות

THE
NCSY BENCHER

A BOOK OF PRAYER AND SONG

Edited and translated by David Olivestone

NCSY IS THE
INTERNATIONAL YOUTH MOVEMENT OF THE ORTHODOX UNION

DOWNLOAD THE NCSY BENCHER APP: NCSY.ORG/BENCHER

Second Revised Edition, 2012.
Seventeenth Printing, 2022.

Copyright © 1982, 1983, 1993, 2012 by Orthodox Union.

English translations copyright © 1982, 1993, 2012 by David Olivestone.

This entire text, the translations, the instructions and the layout, have been written, edited, designed and/or revised as to content, form and style especially for this publication.

All rights reserved. No part of this publication may be reproduced in any form or by any means, including photocopying, without permission in writing from the publisher.

Published by OU/NCSY Publications,
Orthodox Union, 40 Rector Street, New York, NY 10006.
212.563.4000 • www.ou.org.

Download the NCSY Bencher app: ncsybencher.org

Distributed by Mesorah Publications, Inc.,
313 Regina Avenue, Rahway, New Jersey 07065

Distributed in Israel by Sifriati/A. Gitler Books,
Moshav Magshimim, Israel.

Distributed in Europe by Lehmanns,
Unit E, Viking Industrial Park, Rolling Mill Road,
Jarrow, Tyne & Wear NE32 3DP, England.

Distributed in Australia and New Zealand by Golds World of Judaica,
3-13 William Street, Balaclava, Melbourne 3183, Victoria, Australia.

Distributed in South Africa by Kollel Bookshop,
Northfield Centre, 17 Northfield Avenue,
Glenhazel 2192, Johannesburg, South Africa.

ISBN 978-1-879016-38-5 (full color cover)
ISBN 978-1-879016-39-2 (white cover)
ISBN 978-1-879016-52-1 (silver cover)
PRINTED IN THE UNITED STATES OF AMERICA

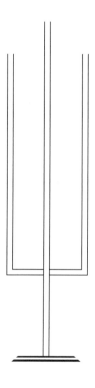

In memory of

Henry I. Rothman ז״ל
and

Bertha G. Rothman ז״ל
לחמו מלחמות ה׳

*"who lived and fought
for Torah-true Judaism"*

Published through the courtesy of the
HENRY, BERTHA AND EDWARD ROTHMAN FOUNDATION
Rochester, NY • Circleville, OH • Cleveland, OH

Guide to Reading the Transliteration

The transliteration in this "Classic" edition of *The NCSY Bencher* follows the Ashkenazic pronunciation of Hebrew. For modern Israeli (Sephardic) transliteration, see the "Ivrit" edition of the *Bencher*.

Consonants are to be read as they sound in English, except for the combination **ch** (ח, כ, ך), which is pronounced as in *challah*.

The "silent" Hebrew letters (א and ע) are not represented.

Vowels are to be pronounced as follows:

a	(ָ)	*as in*	hurr**a**h
o	(ָ)	*as in*	**o**ften
ō	(ֹ)	*as in*	p**o**st
ay	(ֵ)	*as in*	p**ay**
e	(ֶ)	*as in*	l**e**g
i	(ִ)	*as in*	mach**i**ne
u	(ֻ or וּ)	*as in*	l**u**nar
oy	(וֹ)	*as in*	b**oy**
ai	(ַי)	*as in*	**ai**sle

The sounded *sh'va* (ְ) is represented by ' and is pronounced similarly to the indistinct **a** in ag**o**.

CONTENTS תוכן

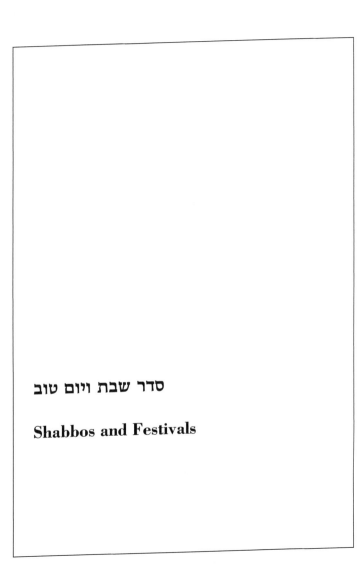

סדר שבת ויום טוב

Shabbos and Festivals

הַדְלָקַת הַנֵּרוֹת לְשַׁבָּת
CANDLE LIGHTING FOR SHABBOS

After lighting the Shabbos candles:

Boruch atoh adōnoy,   בָּרוּךְ אַתָּה יְיָ,

elōhaynu melech ho-ōlom,   אֱלֹהֵינוּ מֶלֶךְ הָעוֹלָם,

asher kid'shonu b'mitzvōsov   אֲשֶׁר קִדְּשָׁנוּ בְּמִצְוֹתָיו

v'tzivonu l'hadlik nayr   וְצִוָּנוּ לְהַדְלִיק נֵר

shel shabbos.   שֶׁל שַׁבָּת.

You are blessed, Lord our God, the sovereign of the world, who made us holy with His commandments and commanded us to kindle lights for Shabbos.

Y'hi rotzōn mil'fonecho, adōnoy   יְהִי רָצוֹן מִלְּפָנֶיךָ, יְיָ

elōhaynu vaylōhay avōsaynu,   אֱלֹהֵינוּ וֵאלֹהֵי אֲבוֹתֵינוּ,

sheyiboneh bays hamikdosh   שֶׁיִּבָּנֶה בֵּית הַמִּקְדָּשׁ

bimhayroh v'yomaynu, v'sayn   בִּמְהֵרָה בְיָמֵינוּ, וְתֵן

chelkaynu b'sōrosecho. V'shom   חֶלְקֵנוּ בְּתוֹרָתֶךָ. וְשָׁם

na-avodcho b'yir-oh kimay   נַעֲבָדְךָ בְּיִרְאָה כִּימֵי

ōlom uchshonim kadmoniyōs.   עוֹלָם וּכְשָׁנִים קַדְמוֹנִיּוֹת.

V'or'voh ladōnoy minchas y'hudoh   וְעָרְבָה לַייָ מִנְחַת יְהוּדָה

virusholo-yim, kimay ōlom   וִירוּשָׁלָיִם, כִּימֵי עוֹלָם

uchshonim kadmōniyōs.   וּכְשָׁנִים קַדְמוֹנִיּוֹת.

May it be Your will, Lord our God and God of our fathers, that the Temple will be rebuilt soon in our time, and grant our involvement with Your Torah. And there we will serve You reverently as in days gone by, in olden times.

Y'hi rotzōn mil'fonecho, adōnoy   יְהִי רָצוֹן מִלְּפָנֶיךָ, יְיָ

elōhai vaylōhay avōsai,   אֱלֹהַי וֵאלֹהֵי אֲבוֹתַי,

shet-chōnayn ōsi (v'es   שֶׁתְּחוֹנֵן אוֹתִי (וְאֶת־

ishi v'es bonai) v'es kol	אִישִׁי וְאֶת־בָּנַי) וְאֶת־כָּל־
k'rōvai v'sashlim botaynu	קְרוֹבַי וְתַשְׁלִים בֵּתֵנוּ
v'sashkayn sh'chinos'cho baynaynu.	וְתַשְׁכֵּן שְׁכִינָתְךָ בֵּינֵינוּ.
V'zakayni l'gadayl bonim uvnay	וְזַכֵּנִי לְגַדֵּל בָּנִים וּבְנֵי
vonim chachomim um-irim	בָנִים חֲכָמִים וּמְאִירִים
es ho-ōlom batōroh	אֶת־הָעוֹלָם בַּתּוֹרָה
uvma-asim tōvim v'ho-ayr	וּבְמַעֲשִׂים טוֹבִים וְהָאֵר
nayraynu shelō yichbeh l'ōlom	נֵרֵנוּ שֶׁלֹּא יִכְבֶּה לְעוֹלָם
vo-ed.V'ho-ayr ponecho v'nivoshay-oh.	וָעֶד. וְהָאֵר פָּנֶיךָ וְנִוָּשֵׁעָה.
Omayn.	אָמֵן.

May it be Your will, Lord my God and God of my fathers, to be gracious to me (and to my husband and children) and to all my family, crowning our home with the feeling of Your divine presence dwelling among us. Make me worthy to raise learned children and grandchildren who will dazzle the world with Torah and goodness, and ensure that the glow of our lives will never be dimmed. Show us the glow of Your face and we will be saved. Amen.

הַדְלָקַת הַנֵּרוֹת לְחַגִּים
CANDLE LIGHTING FOR FESTIVALS

After lighting the candles:

Boruch atoh adōnoy,	בָּרוּךְ אַתָּה יְיָ,
elōhaynu melech ho-ōlom,	אֱלֹהֵינוּ מֶלֶךְ הָעוֹלָם,
asher kid'shonu b'mitzvōsov	אֲשֶׁר קִדְּשָׁנוּ בְּמִצְוֹתָיו
v'tzivonu l'hadlik nayr shel	וְצִוָּנוּ לְהַדְלִיק נֵר שֶׁל
(shabbos v'shel)	(שַׁבָּת וְשֶׁל)
yōm tōv.	יוֹם טוֹב.

You are blessed, Lord our God, the sovereign of the world, who made us with His commandments and commanded us to kindle lights for s and for) the festival.

2

Omit on the last two evenings of Pesach:

Boruch atoh adōnoy,

elōhaynu melech ho-ōlom,

shehecheyonu v'kiy'monu v'higi-onu

laz'man hazeh.

Y'hi rotzōn . . .

בָּרוּךְ אַתָּה יְיָ,
אֱלֹהֵינוּ מֶלֶךְ הָעוֹלָם,
שֶׁהֶחֱיָנוּ וְקִיְּמָנוּ וְהִגִּיעָנוּ
לַזְּמַן הַזֶּה.

יְהִי רָצוֹן . . .

You are blessed, Lord our God, the sovereign of the world, who has kept us alive and sustained us and enabled us to reach this occasion.

May it be Your will. . . .

הַדְלָקַת הַנֵּרוֹת לְיוֹם הַכִּפּוּרִים
CANDLE LIGHTING FOR YOM KIPPUR

After lighting the candles:

Boruch atoh adōnoy,

elōhaynu melech ho-ōlom,

asher kid'shonu b'mitzvōsov

v'tzivonu l'hadlik nayr shel

(shabbos v'shel)

yōm hakipurim.

בָּרוּךְ אַתָּה יְיָ,
אֱלֹהֵינוּ מֶלֶךְ הָעוֹלָם,
אֲשֶׁר קִדְּשָׁנוּ בְּמִצְוֹתָיו
וְצִוָּנוּ לְהַדְלִיק נֵר שֶׁל
(שַׁבָּת וְשֶׁל)
יוֹם הַכִּפּוּרִים.

Boruch atoh adōnoy,

elōhaynu melech ho-ōlom,

shehecheyonu v'kiy'monu v'higi-onu

laz'man hazeh.

Y'hi rotzōn . . .

בָּרוּךְ אַתָּה יְיָ,
אֱלֹהֵינוּ מֶלֶךְ הָעוֹלָם,
שֶׁהֶחֱיָנוּ וְקִיְּמָנוּ וְהִגִּיעָנוּ
לַזְּמַן הַזֶּה.

יְהִי רָצוֹן . . .

You are blessed, Lord our God, the sovereign of the world, who made us holy with His commandments and commanded us to kindle lights for (Shabbos and for) Yom Kippur.

You are blessed, Lord our God, the sovereign of the world, who has kept us alive and sustained us and enabled us to reach this occasion.

May it be Your will . . .

3

שָׁלוֹם עֲלֵיכֶם
SHOLŌM ALAYCHEM

Sholōm alaychem mal-achay
hashorays mal-achay elyōn,
mimelech malchay ham'lochim
hakodōsh boruch hu.

שָׁלוֹם עֲלֵיכֶם מַלְאֲכֵי
הַשָּׁרֵת מַלְאֲכֵי עֶלְיוֹן,
מִמֶּלֶךְ מַלְכֵי הַמְּלָכִים
הַקָּדוֹשׁ בָּרוּךְ הוּא.

Bō-achem l'sholōm mal-achay
hasholōm mal-achay elyōn,
mimelech malchay ham'lochim
hakodōsh boruch hu.

בּוֹאֲכֶם לְשָׁלוֹם מַלְאֲכֵי
הַשָּׁלוֹם מַלְאֲכֵי עֶלְיוֹן,
מִמֶּלֶךְ מַלְכֵי הַמְּלָכִים
הַקָּדוֹשׁ בָּרוּךְ הוּא.

Borchuni l'sholōm mal-achay
hasholōm mal-achay elyōn,
mimelech malchay ham'lochim
hakodōsh boruch hu.

בָּרְכוּנִי לְשָׁלוֹם מַלְאֲכֵי
הַשָּׁלוֹם מַלְאֲכֵי עֶלְיוֹן,
מִמֶּלֶךְ מַלְכֵי הַמְּלָכִים
הַקָּדוֹשׁ בָּרוּךְ הוּא.

Tzays'chem l'sholōm mal-achay
hasholōm mal-achay elyōn,
mimelech malchay ham'lochim
hakodōsh boruch hu.

צֵאתְכֶם לְשָׁלוֹם מַלְאֲכֵי
הַשָּׁלוֹם מַלְאֲכֵי עֶלְיוֹן,
מִמֶּלֶךְ מַלְכֵי הַמְּלָכִים
הַקָּדוֹשׁ בָּרוּךְ הוּא.

Welcome, ministering angels, messengers of the Most High, of the supreme King of Kings, the Holy One, blessed be He.

Come in peace, messengers of peace, messengers of the Most High, of the supreme King of Kings, the Holy One, blessed be He.

Bless me with peace, messengers of peace, messengers of the Most High, of the supreme King of Kings, the Holy One, blessed be He.

And may your departure be in peace, messengers of peace, messengers of the Most High, of the supreme King of Kings, the Holy One, blessed be He.

Ki mal-ochov y'tzaveh loch,

lishmorcho b'chol d'rochecho.

Adōnoy yishmōr tzays'cho

uvō-echo, may-atoh v'ad ōlom.

כִּי מַלְאָכָיו יְצַוֶּה־לָּךְ,

לִשְׁמָרְךָ בְּכָל־דְּרָכֶיךָ. יְיָ

יִשְׁמָר־צֵאתְךָ וּבוֹאֶךָ,

מֵעַתָּה וְעַד־עוֹלָם.

He will command His angels to watch over you in all your ways. The Lord will watch over your comings and goings from now on and forever more.

רִבּוֹן כָּל־הָעוֹלָמִים
RIBŌN KOL HO-ŌLOMIM

Ribōn kol ho-ōlomim, adōn kol

han'shomōs, adōn hasholōm, melech

abir, melech boruch, melech godōl,

melech dōvayr sholōm, melech hodur,

melech vosik, melech zoch, melech chay

ho-ōlomim, melech tōv umaytiv,

melech yochid umyuchod, melech kabir,

melech lōvaysh rachamim, melech

malchay ham'lochim melech nisgov,

melech sōmaych nōf'lim, melech

oseh ma-asayh v'rayshis, melech

pōdeh umatzil, melech tzach v'odōm,

melech kodōsh, melech rom v'niso,

melech shōmay-a t'filoh,

melech tomim darkō.

רִבּוֹן כָּל־הָעוֹלָמִים, אֲדוֹן כָּל־

הַנְּשָׁמוֹת, אֲדוֹן הַשָּׁלוֹם. מֶלֶךְ

אַבִּיר, מֶלֶךְ בָּרוּךְ, מֶלֶךְ גָּדוֹל,

מֶלֶךְ דּוֹבֵר שָׁלוֹם, מֶלֶךְ הָדוּר,

מֶלֶךְ וָתִיק, מֶלֶךְ זַךְ, מֶלֶךְ חֵי

הָעוֹלָמִים, מֶלֶךְ טוֹב וּמֵטִיב,

מֶלֶךְ יָחִיד וּמְיֻחָד, מֶלֶךְ כַּבִּיר,

מֶלֶךְ לוֹבֵשׁ רַחֲמִים, מֶלֶךְ

מַלְכֵי הַמְּלָכִים, מֶלֶךְ נִשְׂגָּב,

מֶלֶךְ סוֹמֵךְ נוֹפְלִים, מֶלֶךְ

עוֹשֶׂה מַעֲשֶׂה בְרֵאשִׁית, מֶלֶךְ

פּוֹדֶה וּמַצִּיל, מֶלֶךְ צַח וְאָדוֹם,

מֶלֶךְ קָדוֹשׁ, מֶלֶךְ רָם וְנִשָּׂא,

מֶלֶךְ שׁוֹמֵעַ תְּפִלָּה,

מֶלֶךְ תָּמִים דַּרְכּוֹ.

Master of all worlds! Lord of all souls! Lord of peace! Mighty King, blessed King, great King, King who is synonymous with peace, glorious King, ancient King, pure King, King who is the life force of the universe, good and beneficent King, unique and singular King, powerful King, King robed in mercy, supreme King of Kings, sublime King, King who sustains the fallen,

King who is the author of creation, King who liberates and rescues, dazzling and ruddied King, holy King, exalted and elevated King, King who hears prayer, King whose way is flawless.

Mōdeh ani l'fonecho, adōnoy elōhai	מוֹדֶה אֲנִי לְפָנֶיךָ יְיָ אֱלֹהַי
vaylōhay avōsai, al kol hachesed	וֵאלֹהֵי אֲבוֹתַי עַל כָּל־הַחֶסֶד
asher osiso imodi, va-asher	אֲשֶׁר עָשִׂיתָ עִמָּדִי, וַאֲשֶׁר
atoh osid la-asōs imi v'im	אַתָּה עָתִיד לַעֲשׂוֹת עִמִּי, וְעִם
kol b'nay vaysi v'im kol	כָּל־בְּנֵי בֵיתִי, וְעִם כָּל־
b'riyosecho, b'nay v'risi. Uvruchim	בְּרִיּוֹתֶיךָ, בְּנֵי בְרִיתִי. וּבְרוּכִים
haym mal-ochecho hak'dōshim	הֵם מַלְאָכֶיךָ הַקְּדוֹשִׁים
v'hat'hōrim she-ōsim r'tzōnecho.	וְהַטְּהוֹרִים שֶׁעוֹשִׂים רְצוֹנֶךָ.
Adōn hasholōm, melech shehasholōm	אֲדוֹן הַשָּׁלוֹם, מֶלֶךְ שֶׁהַשָּׁלוֹם
shelō, bor'chayni vasholōm, v'sifkōd	שֶׁלּוֹ, בָּרְכֵנִי בַשָּׁלוֹם, וְתִפְקוֹד
ōsi v'es kol b'nay vaysi, v'chol	אוֹתִי וְאֶת־כָּל־בְּנֵי בֵיתִי, וְכָל־
am'cho bays yisro-ayl l'cha-yim	עַמְּךָ בֵּית יִשְׂרָאֵל, לְחַיִּים
tōvim ul'sholōm.	טוֹבִים וּלְשָׁלוֹם.

I thank You, Lord my God and God of my fathers, for all the kindness with which You have treated me, and with which You will in the future treat me, my entire household, and all Your creatures who are associated with me. May Your holy and pure angels, who do Your bidding, be blessed. Lord of peace, King to whom peace belongs, bless me with peace, and consider me, my entire household, and all Your people the house of Israel, worthy of a life of well-being and peace.

Melech elyōn al kol tz'vo	מֶלֶךְ עֶלְיוֹן עַל כָּל־צְבָא
morōm, yōtz'raynu, yōtzayr b'rayshis,	מָרוֹם. יוֹצְרֵנוּ, יוֹצֵר בְּרֵאשִׁית,
achaleh fonecho ham'irim,	אֲחַלֶּה פָנֶיךָ הַמְּאִירִים,
shet'zakeh ōsi v'es kol b'nay	שֶׁתְּזַכֶּה אוֹתִי וְאֶת־כָּל־בְּנֵי
vaysi limtzō chayn v'saychel tōv	בֵיתִי לִמְצוֹא חֵן וְשֵׂכֶל טוֹב
b'aynecho uv-aynay chol b'nay odom,	בְּעֵינֶיךָ וּבְעֵינֵי כָל־בְּנֵי אָדָם,
uv-aynay chol rō-aynu, la-avōdosecho.	וּבְעֵינֵי כָל־רוֹאֵינוּ, לַעֲבוֹדָתֶךָ.

V'zakaynu l'kabayl shabbosōs mitōch	וְזַכֵּנוּ לְקַבֵּל שַׁבָּתוֹת מִתּוֹךְ
rōv simchoh, umitōch ōsher	רוֹב שִׂמְחָה, וּמִתּוֹךְ עֹשֶׁר
v'chovōd, umitōch mi-ut avōnōs;	וְכָבוֹד, וּמִתּוֹךְ מִעוּט עֲוֹנוֹת.
v'hosayr mimeni umikol b'nay vaysi,	וְהָסֵר מִמֶּנִּי וּמִכָּל־בְּנֵי בֵיתִי,
umikol amcho bays yisro-ayl, kol	וּמִכָּל־עַמְּךָ בֵּית יִשְׂרָאֵל, כָּל־
minay chōli v'chol minay madveh,	מִינֵי חֹלִי וְכָל־מִינֵי מַדְוֶה,
v'chol minay dalus va-aniyus	וְכָל־מִינֵי דַלּוּת וַעֲנִיּוּת
v'evyōnus; v'sen bonu yaytzer tōv	וְאֶבְיוֹנוּת. וְתֶן בָּנוּ יֵצֶר טוֹב
l'ovd'cho be-emes uv-yiroh	לְעָבְדְּךָ בֶּאֱמֶת וּבְיִרְאָה
uv'ahavoh. V'nih-yeh m'chubodim	וּבְאַהֲבָה. וְנִהְיֶה מְכֻבָּדִים
b'aynecho uv'aynay chol rō-aynu, ki	בְּעֵינֶיךָ וּבְעֵינֵי־כָל־רוֹאֵינוּ כִּי
atoh hu melech hakovōd, ki l'cho	אַתָּה הוּא מֶלֶךְ הַכָּבוֹד, כִּי
no-eh, ki l'cho yo-eh.	לְךָ נָאֶה, כִּי לְךָ יָאֶה.

King who is above the entire heavenly host, our creator, who formed the beginning of all things, I beseech Your resplendent countenance, to grant that I and my entire household find favor and understanding in Your sight, as well as in the sight of all men—all who see us—so that we may serve You. Make us worthy of welcoming Shabbos with great delight, enjoying wealth and respect, and free from too many sins. Keep all kinds of illness, pain, poverty, deprivation and destitution away from me and my entire household. Instill in us a positive desire to serve You with honesty, awe and love. May we command respect in Your sight and in the sight of all who see us, for You are the King of glory, for whom respect is seemly and appropriate.

Ono, melech malchay ham'lochim,	אָנָּא, מֶלֶךְ מַלְכֵי הַמְּלָכִים,
tzavayh l'mal-ochecho, malachay	צַוֵּה לְמַלְאָכֶיךָ, מַלְאֲכֵי
hashorays, m'shorsay elyōn,	הַשָּׁרֵת, מְשָׁרְתֵי עֶלְיוֹן,
sheyifk'duni b'rachamim, vivor'chuni	שֶׁיִּפְקְדוּנִי בְּרַחֲמִים, וִיבָרְכוּנִי
b'vō-om l'vaysi b'yōm kodshaynu.	בְּבוֹאָם לְבֵיתִי בְּיוֹם קָדְשֵׁנוּ.
Ki hidlakti nayrōsai, v'hitzati	כִּי הִדְלַקְתִּי נֵרוֹתַי, וְהִצַּעְתִּי
mitosi, v'hechelafti simlōsai	מִטָּתִי, וְהֶחֱלַפְתִּי שִׂמְלוֹתַי
lichvod yom hashabbos, uvosi	לִכְבוֹד יוֹם הַשַּׁבָּת, וּבָאתִי

l'vays'cho l'hapil t'chinosi l'fonecho	לְבֵיתְךָ לְהַפִּיל תְּחִנָּתִי לְפָנֶיךָ
sheta-avir anchosi, v'o-id asher	שֶׁתַּעֲבִיר אַנְחָתִי, וְאָעִיד אֲשֶׁר
boroso b'shishoh yomim kol	בָּרָאתָ בְּשִׁשָּׁה יָמִים כָּל-
ha-y'tzur; v'eshneh va-ashalaysh ōd	הַיְצוּר, וְאֶשְׁנֶה וַאֲשַׁלֵּשׁ עוֹד
l'ho-id al kōsi b'sōch	לְהָעִיד עַל כּוֹסִי בְּתוֹךְ
simchosi, ka-asher tzivisani l'zochrō	שִׂמְחָתִי, כַּאֲשֶׁר צִוִּיתַנִי לְזָכְרוֹ
ulhisanayg b'yeser nishmosi asher	וּלְהִתְעַנֵּג בְּיֶתֶר נִשְׁמָתִי אֲשֶׁר
nosato bi. Bō eshbōs ka-asher	נָתַתָּ בִּי. בּוֹ אֶשְׁבֹּת כַּאֲשֶׁר
tzivisani l'shor'secho, v'chayn agid	צִוִּיתַנִי לְשָׁרְתֶךָ, וְכֵן אַגִּיד
g'dulos'cho b'rinoh. V'shivisi adōnoy	גְּדֻלָּתְךָ בְּרִנָּה. וְשִׁוִּיתִי יְיָ
likrosi, shet'rachamayni ōd	לְקָרָאתִי, שֶׁתְּרַחֲמֵנִי עוֹד
b'golusi l'go-olayni ul-ōrayr libi	בְּגָלוּתִי לְגָאֳלֵנִי וּלְעוֹרֵר לִבִּי
l'ahavosecho, v'oz eshmōr pikudecho	לְאַהֲבָתֶךָ, וְאָז אֶשְׁמוֹר פִּקּוּדֶיךָ
v'chukecho b'li etzev, v'espalel	וְחֻקֶּיךָ בְּלִי עֶצֶב, וְאֶתְפַּלֵּל
kados, koro-ui uch'nochōn.	כַּדָּת, כָּרָאוּי וּכְנָכוֹן.

   Please, supreme King of Kings, instruct Your messengers, the ministering angels, the messengers of the Most High, to consider me mercifully, blessing me when they visit my house on our holy day. For I kindled my lights, prepared my bed and changed my clothes in honor of Shabbos. I went to Your house to entreat You to banish my tears. I testified that You formed all of creation in six days. Then I repeated it and I will again testify to it a third time over my cup—joyfully—in accordance with your instruction to be mindful of Shabbos, enjoying the additional soul You have given me. I will rest on it, in accordance with Your instruction to serve You, and I will sing Your praises. I have established the Lord as my priority, in order that You should continue to be merciful towards me in my exile by redeeming me and arousing my heart's love for You so that I am able to observe Your bidding and Your laws free from distress, and to say my prayers in accordance with the halachah, appropriately and correctly.

Mal-achay hasholōm, bō-achem	מַלְאֲכֵי הַשָּׁלוֹם, בּוֹאֲכֶם
l'sholōm, bor'chuni l'sholōm,	לְשָׁלוֹם, בָּרְכוּנִי לְשָׁלוֹם,

v'imru boruch l'shulchoni he-oruch,	וְאִמְרוּ בָּרוּךְ לְשֻׁלְחָנִי הֶעָרוּךְ,
v'tzays'chem l'sholōm, may-atoh v'ad	וְצֵאתְכֶם לְשָׁלוֹם, מֵעַתָּה וְעַד
ōlom, omayn seloh.	עוֹלָם, אָמֵן סֶלָה.

Messengers of peace, come in peace, bless me with peace, pronounce a blessing over my Shabbos table, and depart peacefully, now and always. Amen. Selah.

אֵשֶׁת־חַיִל
AYSHES CHA-YIL

Ayshes cha-yil mi yimtzo	אֵשֶׁת־חַיִל מִי יִמְצָא
v'rochōk mip'ninim michroh.	וְרָחֹק מִפְּנִינִים מִכְרָהּ.
Botach boh layv ba-loh	בָּטַח בָּהּ לֵב בַּעְלָהּ
v'sholol lō yechsor.	וְשָׁלָל לֹא יֶחְסָר.
G'molas-hu tōv velō ro kol	גְּמָלַתְהוּ טוֹב וְלֹא־רָע כָּל
y'may cha-yeho. Dor'shoh tzemer	יְמֵי חַיֶּיהָ. דָּרְשָׁה צֶמֶר
ufishtim vata-as b'chayfetz	וּפִשְׁתִּים וַתַּעַשׂ בְּחֵפֶץ
kapeho. Hoy'soh ko-oniyōs	כַּפֶּיהָ. הָיְתָה כָּאֳנִיּוֹת
sōchayr mimerchok tovi	סוֹחֵר מִמֶּרְחָק תָּבִיא
lachmoh. Vatokom b'ōd	לַחְמָהּ. וַתָּקָם בְּעוֹד
lailoh vatitayn teref l'vaysoh	לַיְלָה וַתִּתֵּן טֶרֶף לְבֵיתָהּ
v'chōk l'na-arōseho. Zom'moh	וְחֹק לְנַעֲרֹתֶיהָ. זָמְמָה
sodeh vatikochayhu mip'ri	שָׂדֶה וַתִּקָּחֵהוּ מִפְּרִי
chapeho not'oh korem. Chog'roh	כַפֶּיהָ נָטְעָה כָּרֶם. חָגְרָה
v'ōz mosneho vat-amaytz	בְעוֹז מָתְנֶיהָ וַתְּאַמֵּץ
z'rō-ōseho. To-amoh ki tōv	זְרוֹעֹתֶיהָ. טָעֲמָה כִּי־טוֹב
sachroh lō yichbeh balailoh	סַחְרָהּ לֹא־יִכְבֶּה בַלַּיְלָה
nayroh. Yodeho shil'choh	נֵרָהּ. יָדֶיהָ שִׁלְּחָה
vakishōr v'chapeho tom'chu	בַכִּישׁוֹר וְכַפֶּיהָ תָּמְכוּ

folech. Kapoh por'soh le-oni	פָלֶךְ. כַּפָּה פָּרְשָׂה לֶעָנִי
v'yodeho shil'choh lo-evyōn.	וְיָדֶיהָ שִׁלְּחָה לָאֶבְיוֹן.
Lō siro l'vaysoh misholeg	לֹא-תִירָא לְבֵיתָהּ מִשָּׁלֶג
ki chol baysoh lovush shonim.	כִּי כָל-בֵּיתָהּ לָבֻשׁ שָׁנִים.
Marvadim os'soh loh shaysh	מַרְבַדִּים עָשְׂתָה-לָּהּ שֵׁשׁ
v'argomon l'vushoh. Nōda	וְאַרְגָּמָן לְבוּשָׁהּ. נוֹדָע
bash'orim ba-loh b'shivtō	בַּשְּׁעָרִים בַּעְלָהּ בְּשִׁבְתּוֹ
im ziknay oretz. Sodin	עִם-זִקְנֵי-אָרֶץ. סָדִין
os'soh vatimkōr vachagōr	עָשְׂתָה וַתִּמְכֹּר וַחֲגוֹר
nos'noh lak'na-ani. Ōz v'hodor	נָתְנָה לַכְּנַעֲנִי. עֹז-וְהָדָר
l'vushoh vatis-chak l'yōm	לְבוּשָׁהּ וַתִּשְׂחַק לְיוֹם
acharōn. Piho pos'choh	אַחֲרוֹן. פִּיהָ פָּתְחָה
v'chochmoh v'sōras chesed al	בְחָכְמָה וְתוֹרַת-חֶסֶד עַל
l'shōnoh. Tzōfiyoh halichōs	לְשׁוֹנָהּ. צוֹפִיָּה הֲלִיכוֹת
baysoh v'lechem atzlus lō	בֵּיתָהּ וְלֶחֶם עַצְלוּת לֹא
sōchayl. Komu voneho	תֹאכֵל. קָמוּ בָנֶיהָ
vai-ash'ruho ba-loh vai-hal'loh.	וַיְאַשְּׁרוּהָ בַּעְלָהּ וַיְהַלְלָהּ.
Rabōs bonōs osu cho-yil	רַבּוֹת בָּנוֹת עָשׂוּ חָיִל
v'at olis al kulonoh.	וְאַתְּ עָלִית עַל-כֻּלָּנָה.
Sheker hachayn v'hevel hayōfi	שֶׁקֶר הַחֵן וְהֶבֶל הַיֹּפִי
ishoh yir-as adōnoy hi	אִשָּׁה יִרְאַת-יְיָ הִיא
sis-halol. T'nu loh mip'ri	תִתְהַלָּל. תְּנוּ-לָהּ מִפְּרִי
yodeho vihal'luho vash'orim	יָדֶיהָ וִיהַלְלוּהָ בַשְּׁעָרִים
ma-aseho.	מַעֲשֶׂיהָ.

A good wife who can find? She is more precious than corals. Her husband places his trust in her and only profits thereby. She brings him good, not harm, all the days of her life. She seeks out wool and flax and cheerfully does the work of her hands. She is like the trading ships, bringing food from afar. She gets up while it is still night to provide food for her household, and a fair share for her staff. She considers a field and purchases it and plants a vineyard with the fruit of her labors. She invests herself with strength and makes her arms powerful. She senses that her trade is profitable; her light does not go out at night. She stretches out her hands to the distaff and her palms hold the spindle. She opens her hand to the poor and reaches out her hands to the needy. She has no fear of the snow for her household, for all her household is dressed in fine clothing. She makes her own coverlets; her clothing is of fine linen and luxurious cloth. Her husband is known at the gates, where he sits with the elders of the land. She makes and sells linens; she supplies the merchants with sashes. She is robed in strength and dignity and she smiles at the future. She opens her mouth with wisdom and the teaching of kindness is on her tongue. She looks after the conduct of her household and never tastes the bread of sloth. Her children rise up and make her happy; her husband praises her: "Many women have excelled, but you outshine them all!" Grace is elusive and beauty is vain, but a woman who fears the Lord—she shall be praised. Give her credit for the fruit of her labors and let her achievements praise her at the gates.

בִּרְכַּת הַבָּנִים
BLESSING THE CHILDREN

For a son:

Y'sim'cho elōhim
k'efra-yim v'chimnasheh.

יְשִׂמְךָ אֱלֹהִים
כְּאֶפְרַיִם וְכִמְנַשֶּׁה.

May God make you like Ephraim and Menasseh.

For a daughter:

Y'simaych elōhim k'soroh,
rivkoh, rochayl v'lay-oh.

יְשִׂמֵךְ אֱלֹהִים כְּשָׂרָה,
רִבְקָה, רָחֵל וְלֵאָה.

May God make you like Sarah, Rebecca, Rachel and Leah.

For both continue:

Y'vorech'cho adōnoy v'yishm'recho.
Yo-ayr adōnoy ponov aylecho vichuneko.
Yiso adōnoy ponov aylecho,
v'yosaym l'cho sholōm.

יְבָרֶכְךָ יְיָ וְיִשְׁמְרֶךָ.
יָאֵר יְיָ פָּנָיו אֵלֶיךָ וִיחֻנֶּךָ.
יִשָּׂא יְיָ פָּנָיו אֵלֶיךָ,
וְיָשֵׂם לְךָ שָׁלוֹם.

May the Lord bless you and watch over you. May the Lord shine His face towards you and show you favor. May the Lord be favorably disposed towards you and may He grant you peace.

11

קִדּוּשׁ לְלֵיל שַׁבָּת
KIDDUSH FOR FRIDAY EVENING

Kiddush is recited over a full cup of wine.

Vai-hi erev vai-hi vōker
yōm hashishi.

וַיְהִי־עֶרֶב וַיְהִי־בֹקֶר
יוֹם הַשִּׁשִּׁי.

Vai-chulu hashoma-yim v'ho-oretz
v'chol tz'vo-om. Vai-chal
elōhim bayōm hash'vi-i
m'lachtō asher osoh,
va-yishbōs ba-yōm hash'vi-i
mikol m'lachtō asher
osoh. Vai-vorech elōhim
es yōm hash'vi-i vai-kadaysh
ōsō, ki vō shovas mikol
m'lachtō asher boro
elōhim la-asōs.

וַיְכֻלּוּ הַשָּׁמַיִם וְהָאָרֶץ
וְכָל־צְבָאָם. וַיְכַל
אֱלֹהִים בַּיּוֹם הַשְּׁבִיעִי
מְלַאכְתּוֹ אֲשֶׁר עָשָׂה,
וַיִּשְׁבֹּת בַּיּוֹם הַשְּׁבִיעִי
מִכָּל־מְלַאכְתּוֹ אֲשֶׁר
עָשָׂה. וַיְבָרֶךְ אֱלֹהִים
אֶת־יוֹם הַשְּׁבִיעִי וַיְקַדֵּשׁ
אוֹתוֹ, כִּי בוֹ שָׁבַת מִכָּל־
מְלַאכְתּוֹ אֲשֶׁר בָּרָא
אֱלֹהִים לַעֲשׂוֹת.

It was evening and it was morning, the sixth day. So the heavens and the earth were finished, with all their complement. Thus, on the seventh day, God had completed His work which He had undertaken, and He rested on the seventh day from all His work which He had been doing. Then God blessed the seventh day and made it holy, because on it He rested from all His creative work, which God had brought into being to fulfill its purpose.

Savray mōronon v'rabonon v'rabōsai:

סָבְרִי מָרָנָן וְרַבָּנָן וְרַבּוֹתָי:

Boruch atoh adōnoy,
elōhaynu melech ho-ōlom,
bōray p'ri hagofen.

בָּרוּךְ אַתָּה יְיָ,
אֱלֹהֵינוּ מֶלֶךְ הָעוֹלָם,
בּוֹרֵא פְּרִי הַגָּפֶן.

You are blessed, Lord our God, the sovereign of the world, creator of the fruit of the vine.

Boruch atoh adōnoy,	בָּרוּךְ אַתָּה יְיָ,
elōhaynu melech ho-ōlom,	אֱלֹהֵינוּ מֶלֶךְ הָעוֹלָם,
asher kid'shonu b'mitzvōsov	אֲשֶׁר קִדְּשָׁנוּ בְּמִצְוֹתָיו
v'rotzoh vonu, v'shabbos kodshō	וְרָצָה בָנוּ, וְשַׁבַּת קָדְשׁוֹ
b'ahavoh uvrotzōn hinchilonu,	בְּאַהֲבָה וּבְרָצוֹן הִנְחִילָנוּ,
zikorōn l'ma-asayh v'rayshis.	זִכָּרוֹן לְמַעֲשֵׂה בְרֵאשִׁית.
Ki hu yōm t'chiloh	כִּי הוּא יוֹם תְּחִלָּה
l'mikro-ay kōdesh, zaycher	לְמִקְרָאֵי קֹדֶשׁ, זֵכֶר
litzi-as mitzro-yim. Ki vonu	לִיצִיאַת מִצְרָיִם. כִּי־בָנוּ
vocharto v'ōsonu kidashto	בָחַרְתָּ וְאוֹתָנוּ קִדַּשְׁתָּ
mikol ho-amim, v'shabbos	מִכָּל־הָעַמִּים, וְשַׁבַּת
kodsh'cho b'ahavoh uvrotzōn	קָדְשְׁךָ בְּאַהֲבָה וּבְרָצוֹן
hinchaltonu. Boruch atoh adōnoy,	הִנְחַלְתָּנוּ. בָּרוּךְ אַתָּה יְיָ,
m'kadaysh hashabbos.	מְקַדֵּשׁ הַשַּׁבָּת.

You are blessed, Lord our God, the sovereign of the world, who made us holy with His commandments and favored us, and gave us His holy Shabbos, in love and favor, to be our heritage, as a reminder of the Creation. It is the foremost day of the holy festivals marking the exodus from Egypt. For—out of all the nations—You chose us and made us holy, and You gave us Your holy Shabbos, in love and favor, as our heritage. You are blessed, Lord, who sanctifies Shabbos.

קִדּוּשׁ לְלֵיל יוֹם טוֹב
KIDDUSH FOR FESTIVAL EVENINGS

Kiddush is recited over a full cup of wine.

On Shabbos begin here:

Vai-hi erev vai-hi võker
yõm hashishi.

וַיְהִי־עֶרֶב וַיְהִי־בֹקֶר
יוֹם הַשִּׁשִּׁי.

Vai-chulu hashoma-yim v'ho-oretz
v'chol tz'vo-om. Vai-chal
elōhim bayōm hash'vi-i
m'lachtō asher osoh,
va-yishbōs ba-yōm hash'vi-i
mikol m'lachtō asher
osoh. Vai-vorech elōhim
es yōm hash'vi-i vai-kadaysh
ōsō, ki vō shovas mikol
m'lachtō asher boro
elōhim la-asōs.

וַיְכֻלּוּ הַשָּׁמַיִם וְהָאָרֶץ
וְכָל־צְבָאָם. וַיְכַל
אֱלֹהִים בַּיּוֹם הַשְּׁבִיעִי
מְלַאכְתּוֹ אֲשֶׁר עָשָׂה,
וַיִּשְׁבֹּת בַּיּוֹם הַשְּׁבִיעִי
מִכָּל־מְלַאכְתּוֹ אֲשֶׁר
עָשָׂה. וַיְבָרֶךְ אֱלֹהִים
אֶת־יוֹם הַשְּׁבִיעִי וַיְקַדֵּשׁ
אוֹתוֹ, כִּי בוֹ שָׁבַת מִכָּל־
מְלַאכְתּוֹ אֲשֶׁר בָּרָא
אֱלֹהִים לַעֲשׂוֹת.

It was evening and it was morning, the sixth day. So the heavens and the earth were finished, with all their complement. Thus, on the seventh day, God had completed His work which He had undertaken, and He rested on the seventh day from all His work which He had been doing. Then God blessed the seventh day and made it holy, because on it He rested from all His creative work, which God had brought into being to fulfill its purpose.

On other evenings begin here:

Sovray moronon v'rabonon v'rabōsai:

סָבְרִי מָרָנָן וְרַבָּנָן וְרַבּוֹתַי:

Boruch atoh adōnoy,
elōhaynu melech ho-ōlom,
bōray p'ri hagofen.

בָּרוּךְ אַתָּה יְיָ,
אֱלֹהֵינוּ מֶלֶךְ הָעוֹלָם,
בּוֹרֵא פְּרִי הַגָּפֶן.

14

You are blessed, Lord our God, the sovereign of the world, creator of the fruit of the vine.

Boruch atoh adōnoy,	בָּרוּךְ אַתָּה יְיָ,
elōhaynu melech ho-ōlom,	אֱלֹהֵינוּ מֶלֶךְ הָעוֹלָם,
asher bochar bonu mikol om,	אֲשֶׁר בָּחַר בָּנוּ מִכָּל-עָם,
v'rōm'monu mikol loshōn,	וְרוֹמְמָנוּ מִכָּל-לָשׁוֹן,
v'kid'shonu b'mitzvōsov.	וְקִדְּשָׁנוּ בְּמִצְוֹתָיו.
Vatiten lonu, adōnoy	וַתִּתֶּן-לָנוּ, יְיָ
elōhaynu, b'ahavoh	אֱלֹהֵינוּ, בְּאַהֲבָה
(shabbosōs limnuchoh u)	(שַׁבָּתוֹת לִמְנוּחָה וּ)
mō-adim l'simchoh, chagim	מוֹעֲדִים לְשִׂמְחָה, חַגִּים
uzmanim l'sosōn, es yōm	וּזְמַנִּים לְשָׂשׂוֹן, אֶת-יוֹם
(hashabbos hazeh, v'es yōm)	(הַשַּׁבָּת הַזֶּה, וְאֶת-יוֹם)

on Pesach

chag hamatzōs hazeh,	חַג הַמַּצּוֹת הַזֶּה,
z'man chayrusaynu,	זְמַן חֵרוּתֵנוּ,

on Shavuos

chag hashovu-ōs hazeh,	חַג הַשָּׁבֻעוֹת הַזֶּה,
z'man matan tōrosaynu,	זְמַן מַתַּן תּוֹרָתֵינוּ,

on Sukkos

chag hasukkōs hazeh,	חַג הַסֻּכּוֹת הַזֶּה,
z'man simchosaynu	זְמַן שִׂמְחָתֵנוּ

on Sh'mini Atzeres and Simchas Torah

hash'mini, chag ho-atzeres	הַשְּׁמִינִי, חַג הָעֲצֶרֶת
hazeh, z'man simchosaynu,	הַזֶּה, זְמַן שִׂמְחָתֵנוּ,
(b'ahavoh) mikro kōdesh,	(בְּאַהֲבָה) מִקְרָא קֹדֶשׁ,
zaycher litzi-as mitzroyim. Ki	זֵכֶר לִיצִיאַת מִצְרָיִם. כִּי־
vonu vocharto v'ōsonu kidashto	בָנוּ בָחַרְתָּ וְאוֹתָנוּ קִדַּשְׁתָּ

mikol ho-amim, (v'shabbos)	מִכָּל־הָעַמִּים, (וְשַׁבָּת)
umō-aday kodsh'cho (b'ahavoh	וּמוֹעֲדֵי קָדְשֶׁךָ (בְּאַהֲבָה
uvrotzōn) b'simchoh uvsosōn	וּבְרָצוֹן) בְּשִׂמְחָה וּבְשָׂשׂוֹן
hinchaltonu. Boruch atoh adōnoy,	הִנְחַלְתָּנוּ. בָּרוּךְ אַתָּה יְיָ,
m'kadaysh (hashabbos v')	מְקַדֵּשׁ (הַשַּׁבָּת וְ)
yisro-ayl v'haz'manim.	יִשְׂרָאֵל וְהַזְּמַנִּים.

You are blessed, Lord our God, the sovereign of the world, who chose us out of all the nations, and exalted us above all peoples, and made us holy with His commandments. You gave us, Lord our God, with love (Shabbos for rest and) set times for joy, festivals and holidays for happiness: this (Shabbos and this) Festival day of

Pesach/Shavuos/Sukkos/Sh'mini Atzeres

(with love), a sacred assembly marking the exodus from Egypt. For—out of all the nations—You chose us and made us holy, and You gave us Your holy (Shabbos and) festivals (in love and favor) for joy and for happiness, as our heritage. You are blessed, Lord, who sanctifies (Shabbos,) Israel and the holidays.

On Saturday night add:

Boruch atoh adōnoy,	בָּרוּךְ אַתָּה יְיָ,
elōhaynu melech ho-ōlom,	אֱלֹהֵינוּ מֶלֶךְ הָעוֹלָם,
bōray m'ōray ho-aysh.	בּוֹרֵא מְאוֹרֵי הָאֵשׁ.

You are blessed, Lord our God, the sovereign of the world, creator of the lights of fire.

Boruch atoh adōnoy,	בָּרוּךְ אַתָּה יְיָ,
elōhaynu melech ho-ōlom,	אֱלֹהֵינוּ מֶלֶךְ הָעוֹלָם,
hamavdil bayn kōdesh l'chōl,	הַמַּבְדִּיל בֵּין קֹדֶשׁ לְחֹל,
bayn ōr l'chōshech, bayn	בֵּין אוֹר לְחֹשֶׁךְ, בֵּין
yisro-ayl lo-amim, bayn yōm	יִשְׂרָאֵל לָעַמִּים, בֵּין יוֹם
hash'vi-i l'shayshes y'may	הַשְּׁבִיעִי לְשֵׁשֶׁת יְמֵי
hama-aseh. Bayn k'dushas	הַמַּעֲשֶׂה. בֵּין קְדֻשַּׁת
shabbos likdushas yōm tōv	שַׁבָּת לִקְדֻשַּׁת יוֹם טוֹב

hivdalto, v'es yōm	הִבְדַּלְתָּ, וְאֶת־יוֹם
hash'vi-i mishayshes y'may	הַשְּׁבִיעִי מִשֵּׁשֶׁת יְמֵי
hama-aseh kidashto. Hivdalto	הַמַּעֲשֶׂה קִדַּשְׁתָּ. הִבְדַּלְתָּ
v'kidashto es am'cho yisro-ayl	וְקִדַּשְׁתָּ אֶת־עַמְּךָ יִשְׂרָאֵל
bikdushosecho. Boruch atoh adōnoy,	בִּקְדֻשָּׁתֶךָ. בָּרוּךְ אַתָּה יְיָ,
hamavdil bayn kōdesh l'kōdesh.	הַמַּבְדִּיל בֵּין קֹדֶשׁ לְקֹדֶשׁ.

You are blessed, Lord our God, the sovereign of the world, who makes a distinction between sacred and secular, between light and darkness, between Israel and the other nations, between the seventh day and the six working days. You made a distinction between the holiness of Shabbos and the holiness of a festival, just as You made the seventh day holier than the six working days. You have set levels of holiness for Your people Israel through Your sanctity. You are blessed, Lord, who sets different levels of holiness.

Omit on the last two evenings of Pesach:

Boruch atoh adōnoy,	בָּרוּךְ אַתָּה יְיָ,
elōhaynu melech ho-ōlom,	אֱלֹהֵינוּ מֶלֶךְ הָעוֹלָם,
shehecheyonu v'kiy'monu v'higi-onu	שֶׁהֶחֱיָנוּ וְקִיְּמָנוּ וְהִגִּיעָנוּ
laz'man hazeh.	לַזְּמַן הַזֶּה.

You are blessed, Lord our God, the sovereign of the world, who has kept us alive and sustained us and enabled us to reach this occasion.

In the sukkah add:

Boruch atoh adōnoy,	בָּרוּךְ אַתָּה יְיָ,
elōhaynu melech ho-ōlom,	אֱלֹהֵינוּ מֶלֶךְ הָעוֹלָם,
asher kid'shonu b'mitzvōsov	אֲשֶׁר קִדְּשָׁנוּ בְּמִצְוֹתָיו
v'tzivonu layshayv basukkoh.	וְצִוָּנוּ לֵישֵׁב בַּסֻּכָּה.

You are blessed, Lord our God, the sovereign of the world, who made us holy with His commandments and commanded us to live in the sukkah.

(On the first evening of Sukkos only, say this blessing
***before** the preceding one.)*

קִדּוּשׁ לְלֵיל רֹאשׁ הַשָּׁנָה
KIDDUSH FOR ROSH HASHANAH EVENING

Kiddush is recited over a full cup of wine.

On Shabbos begin here:

Vai-hi erev vai-hi vōker	וַיְהִי־עֶרֶב וַיְהִי־בֹקֶר
yōm hashishi.	יוֹם הַשִּׁשִּׁי.
Vai-chulu hashoma-yim v'ho-oretz	וַיְכֻלּוּ הַשָּׁמַיִם וְהָאָרֶץ
v'chol tz'vo-om. Vai-chal	וְכָל־צְבָאָם. וַיְכַל
elōhim bayōm hash'vi-i	אֱלֹהִים בַּיּוֹם הַשְּׁבִיעִי
m'lachtō asher osoh,	מְלַאכְתּוֹ אֲשֶׁר עָשָׂה,
va-yishbōs ba-yōm hash'vi-i	וַיִּשְׁבֹּת בַּיּוֹם הַשְּׁבִיעִי
mikol m'lachtō asher	מִכָּל־מְלַאכְתּוֹ אֲשֶׁר
osoh. Vai-vorech elōhim	עָשָׂה. וַיְבָרֶךְ אֱלֹהִים
es yōm hash'vi-i vai-kadaysh	אֶת־יוֹם הַשְּׁבִיעִי וַיְקַדֵּשׁ
ōsō, ki vō shovas mikol	אֹתוֹ, כִּי בוֹ שָׁבַת מִכָּל־
m'lachtō asher boro	מְלַאכְתּוֹ אֲשֶׁר בָּרָא
elōhim la-asōs.	אֱלֹהִים לַעֲשׂוֹת.

It was evening and it was morning, the sixth day. So the heavens and the earth were finished, with all their complement. Thus, on the seventh day, God had completed His work which He had undertaken, and He rested on the seventh day from all His work which He had been doing. Then God blessed the seventh day and made it holy, because on it He rested from all His creative work, which God had brought into being to fulfill its purpose.

On other evenings begin here:

Sovray moronon v'rabonon v'rabōsai:	סָבְרִי מָרָנָן וְרַבָּנָן וְרַבּוֹתַי:
Boruch atoh adōnoy,	בָּרוּךְ אַתָּה יְיָ,
elōhaynu melech ho-ōlom,	אֱלֹהֵינוּ מֶלֶךְ הָעוֹלָם,
bōray p'ri hagofen.	בּוֹרֵא פְּרִי הַגָּפֶן.

18

You are blessed, Lord our God, the sovereign of the world, creator of the fruit of the vine.

Boruch atoh adōnoy,	בָּרוּךְ אַתָּה יְיָ,
elōhaynu melech ho-ōlom,	אֱלֹהֵינוּ מֶלֶךְ הָעוֹלָם,
asher bochar bonu mikol om,	אֲשֶׁר בָּחַר בָּנוּ מִכָּל־עָם,
v'rōm'monu mikol loshōn,	וְרוֹמְמָנוּ מִכָּל־לָשׁוֹן,
v'kid'shonu b'mitzvōsov.	וְקִדְּשָׁנוּ בְּמִצְוֺתָיו.
Vatiten lonu, adōnoy	וַתִּתֶּן־לָנוּ, יְיָ
elōhaynu, b'ahavoh es yōm	אֱלֹהֵינוּ, בְּאַהֲבָה אֶת־יוֹם
(hashabbos hazeh v'es yōm)	(הַשַּׁבָּת הַזֶּה וְאֶת־יוֹם)
hazikorōn hazeh, yōm (zichrōn)	הַזִּכָּרוֹן הַזֶּה, יוֹם (זִכְרוֹן)
t'ru-oh (b'ahavoh) mikro	תְּרוּעָה (בְּאַהֲבָה) מִקְרָא
kōdesh, zaycher litzi-as	קֹדֶשׁ, זֵכֶר לִיצִיאַת
mitzro-yim. Ki vonu vocharto	מִצְרָיִם. כִּי־בָנוּ בָחַרְתָּ
v'ōsonu kidashto mikol	וְאוֹתָנוּ קִדַּשְׁתָּ מִכָּל־
ho-amim, udvor'cho emes	הָעַמִּים, וּדְבָרְךָ אֱמֶת
v'kayom lo-ad. Boruch atoh adōnoy,	וְקַיָּם לָעַד. בָּרוּךְ אַתָּה יְיָ,
melech al kol ho-oretz,	מֶלֶךְ עַל כָּל־הָאָרֶץ,
m'kadaysh (haShabbos v')	מְקַדֵּשׁ (הַשַּׁבָּת וְ)
yisro-ayl v'yōm hazikorōn.	יִשְׂרָאֵל וְיוֹם הַזִּכָּרוֹן.

You are blessed, Lord our God, the sovereign of the world, who chose us out of all the nations, and exalted us above all peoples, and made us holy with His commandments. You gave us, Lord our God, with love this (Shabbos day and this) Day of Remembrance, a day for (mentioning) blowing the shofar, a sacred assembly marking the exodus from Egypt. For—out of all the nations—You chose us and made us holy, and your word is true and reliable forever. You are blessed, Lord, the king of the whole earth who sanctifies (Shabbos) Israel and the Day of Remembrance.

On Saturday night add:

Boruch atoh adōnoy,	בָּרוּךְ אַתָּה יְיָ,
elōhaynu melech ho-ōlom,	אֱלֹהֵינוּ מֶלֶךְ הָעוֹלָם,
bōray m'ōray ho-aysh.	בּוֹרֵא מְאוֹרֵי הָאֵשׁ.

You are blessed, Lord our God, the sovereign of the world, creator of the lights of fire.

Boruch atoh adōnoy,	בָּרוּךְ אַתָּה יְיָ,
elōhaynu melech ho-ōlom,	אֱלֹהֵינוּ מֶלֶךְ הָעוֹלָם,
hamavdil bayn kōdesh l'chōl,	הַמַּבְדִּיל בֵּין קֹדֶשׁ לְחֹל,
bayn ōr l'chōshech,	בֵּין אוֹר לְחֹשֶׁךְ,
bayn yisro-ayl lo-amim,	בֵּין יִשְׂרָאֵל לָעַמִּים,
bayn yōm hash'vi-i	בֵּין יוֹם הַשְּׁבִיעִי
l'shayshes y'may hama-aseh. Bayn	לְשֵׁשֶׁת יְמֵי הַמַּעֲשֶׂה. בֵּין
k'dushas shabbos likdushas yōm	קְדֻשַּׁת שַׁבָּת לִקְדֻשַּׁת יוֹם
tōv hivdalto, v'es yōm	טוֹב הִבְדַּלְתָּ, וְאֶת־יוֹם
hash'vi-i mishayshes y'may	הַשְּׁבִיעִי מִשֵּׁשֶׁת יְמֵי
hama-aseh kidashto. Hivdalto	הַמַּעֲשֶׂה קִדַּשְׁתָּ. הִבְדַּלְתָּ
v'kidashto es am'cho yisro-ayl	וְקִדַּשְׁתָּ אֶת־עַמְּךָ יִשְׂרָאֵל
bikdushosecho. Boruch atoh adōnoy,	בִּקְדֻשָּׁתֶךָ. בָּרוּךְ אַתָּה יְיָ,
hamavdil bayn kōdesh l'kōdesh.	הַמַּבְדִּיל בֵּין קֹדֶשׁ לְקֹדֶשׁ.

You are blessed, Lord our God, the sovereign of the world, who makes a distinction between sacred and secular, between light and darkness, between Israel and the other nations, between the seventh day and the six working days. You made a distinction between the holiness of Shabbos and the holiness of a festival, just as You made the seventh day holier than the six working days. You have set levels of holiness for Your people Israel through Your sanctity. You are blessed, Lord, who sets different levels of holiness.

On both evenings continue here:

Boruch atoh adōnoy,	בָּרוּךְ אַתָּה יְיָ,
elohaynu melech ho-ōlom,	אֱלֹהֵינוּ מֶלֶךְ הָעוֹלָם,

shehecheyonu v'kiy'monu v'higi-onu	שֶׁהֶחֱיָנוּ וְקִיְּמָנוּ וְהִגִּיעָנוּ
laz'man hazeh.	לַזְּמַן הַזֶּה.

You are blessed, Lord our God, the sovereign of the world, who has kept us alive and sustained us and enabled us to reach this occasion.

Following Kiddush there is a custom to eat a piece of apple dipped in honey, expressing the wish that the New Year should be a sweet one.

Boruch atoh adōnoy,	בָּרוּךְ אַתָּה יְיָ,
elōhaynu melech ho-ōlom,	אֱלֹהֵינוּ מֶלֶךְ הָעוֹלָם,
bōray p'ri ho-aytz.	בּוֹרֵא פְּרִי הָעֵץ.

You are blessed, Lord our God, the sovereign of the world, creator of the fruit of trees.

After eating some of the apple, say the following:

Y'hi rotzōn mil'fonecho adōnoy	יְהִי רָצוֹן מִלְּפָנֶיךָ יְיָ
elōhaynu vaylōhay avōsaynu	אֱלֹהֵינוּ וֵאלֹהֵי אֲבוֹתֵינוּ
shet'chadaysh olaynu shonoh	שֶׁתְּחַדֵּשׁ עָלֵינוּ שָׁנָה
tōvoh umsukoh.	טוֹבָה וּמְתוּקָה.

May it be Your will, Lord our God and God of our fathers, that You give us a good and sweet New Year.

קִדוּשָׁא רַבָּה לְשַׁבָּת
KIDDUSH FOR SHABBOS MORNING

V'shom'ru v'nay yisro-ayl	וְשָׁמְרוּ בְנֵי־יִשְׂרָאֵל
es hashabbos, la-asōs	אֶת־הַשַּׁבָּת, לַעֲשׂוֹת
es hashabbos l'dōrōsom b'ris	אֶת־הַשַּׁבָּת לְדֹרֹתָם בְּרִית
ōlom. Bayni uvayn	עוֹלָם. בֵּינִי וּבֵין
b'nay yisro-ayl ōs hi	בְּנֵי־יִשְׂרָאֵל אוֹת הִיא
l'ōlom, ki shayshes yomim	לְעוֹלָם, כִּי שֵׁשֶׁת יָמִים
osoh adōnoy es hashoma-yim	עָשָׂה יְיָ אֶת־הַשָּׁמַיִם
v'es ho-oretz uva-yōm	וְאֶת־הָאָרֶץ וּבַיּוֹם
hash'vi-i shovas va-yinofash.	הַשְּׁבִיעִי שָׁבַת וַיִּנָּפַשׁ.

Zochōr es yōm hashabbos	זָכוֹר אֶת־יוֹם הַשַּׁבָּת
l'kad'shō. Shayshes yomim	לְקַדְּשׁוֹ. שֵׁשֶׁת יָמִים
ta-avōd v'osiso kol	תַּעֲבֹד וְעָשִׂיתָ כָּל־
m'lachtecho. V'yōm hash'vi-i	מְלַאכְתֶּךָ. וְיוֹם הַשְּׁבִיעִי
shabbos ladōnoy elōhecho, lō	שַׁבָּת לַייָ אֱלֹהֶיךָ, לֹא־
sa-aseh chol m'lochoh atoh	תַעֲשֶׂה כָל־מְלָאכָה אַתָּה
uvincho uvitecho avd'cho va-amos'cho	וּבִנְךָ וּבִתֶּךָ עַבְדְּךָ וַאֲמָתְךָ
uvhemtecho v'gayr'cho asher	וּבְהֶמְתֶּךָ וְגֵרְךָ אֲשֶׁר
bish-orecho. Ki shayshes yomim	בִּשְׁעָרֶיךָ. כִּי שֵׁשֶׁת־יָמִים
osoh adōnoy es hashoma-yim	עָשָׂה יְיָ אֶת־הַשָּׁמַיִם
v'es ho-oretz es ha-yom	וְאֶת־הָאָרֶץ אֶת־הַיָּם
v'es kol asher bom, va-yonach	וְאֶת־כָּל־אֲשֶׁר־בָּם וַיָּנַח
ba-yōm hash'vi-i,	בַּיּוֹם הַשְּׁבִיעִי,

al kayn bayrach adōnoy es yōm	עַל־כֵּן בֵּרַךְ יְיָ אֶת־יוֹם
hashabbos vai-kad'shayhu.	הַשַּׁבָּת וַיְקַדְּשֵׁהוּ.

The children of Israel should keep Shabbos, observing Shabbos throughout their generations, as an everlasting covenant. It is a sign between Me and
the children of Israel for all time, that in six days the Lord made the heavens
and the earth, and that on the seventh day He was finished and He rested.

Be mindful of Shabbos, to make it holy. You should labor for six days and
do all your work, but the seventh day is Shabbos for the Lord your God.
You may not do any creative work—neither you, not your son, nor your
daughter, nor your male or female worker, nor your cattle, nor the stranger
who dwells among you. Because it was in six days that the Lord made the
heavens and the earth, the sea, and all that they contain, and He rested on
the seventh day.

That is why the Lord blessed Shabbos and made it holy.

Sovray moronon v'rabonon v'rabōsai: :סָבְרֵי מָרָנָן וְרַבָּנָן וְרַבּוֹתַי

For wine:

Boruch atoh adōnoy,   ,בָּרוּךְ אַתָּה יְיָ
elōhaynu melech ho-ōlōm,   ,אֱלֹהֵינוּ מֶלֶךְ הָעוֹלָם
bōray p'ri hagofen.   .בּוֹרֵא פְּרִי הַגָּפֶן

You are blessed, Lord our God, the sovereign of the world, creator of the
fruit of the vine.

For other drinks:

Boruch atoh adōnoy,   ,בָּרוּךְ אַתָּה יְיָ
elōhaynu melech ho-ōlōm,   ,אֱלֹהֵינוּ מֶלֶךְ הָעוֹלָם
shehakōl nihyeh bidvorō.   .שֶׁהַכֹּל נִהְיֶה בִּדְבָרוֹ

You are blessed, Lord our God, the sovereign of the world, through whose
word everything came into being.

קִדוּשָׁא רַבָּה לְשָׁלֹשׁ רְגָלִים וּלְרֹאשׁ הַשָּׁנָה
KIDDUSH FOR FESTIVAL AND
ROSH HASHANAH MORNINGS

On Shabbos begin here:

V'shom'ru v'nay yisro-ayl	וְשָׁמְרוּ בְנֵי־יִשְׂרָאֵל
es hashabbos, la-asōs	אֶת־הַשַׁבָּת, לַעֲשׂוֹת
es hashabbos l'dōrōsom b'ris	אֶת־הַשַׁבָּת לְדֹרֹתָם בְּרִית
ōlom. Bayni uvayn	עוֹלָם. בֵּינִי וּבֵין
b'nay yisro-ayl ōs hi	בְּנֵי־יִשְׂרָאֵל אוֹת הִיא
l'ōlom, ki shayshes yomim	לְעוֹלָם, כִּי שֵׁשֶׁת יָמִים
osoh adōnoy es hashoma-yim	עָשָׂה יְיָ אֶת־הַשָּׁמַיִם
v'es ho-oretz uva-yōm	וְאֶת־הָאָרֶץ וּבַיּוֹם
hash'vi-i shovas va-yinofash.	הַשְּׁבִיעִי שָׁבַת וַיִּנָּפַשׁ.

The children of Israel should keep Shabbos, observing Shabbos throughout their generations, as an everlasting covenant. It is a sign between Me and
the children of Israel for all time, that in six days the Lord made the heavens
and the earth, and that on the seventh day He was finished and He rested.

On a weekday begin here:

For Pesach, Shavuos, Sukkos, Sh'mini Atzeres and Simchas Torah

Ayleh mō-aday adōnoy, mikro-ay	אֵלֶּה מוֹעֲדֵי יְיָ, מִקְרָאֵי
kōdesh, asher tikr'u	קֹדֶשׁ, אֲשֶׁר תִּקְרְאוּ
ōsom b'mō-adom. Vai-dabayr	אוֹתָם בְּמוֹעֲדָם. וַיְדַבֵּר
mōsheh es mō-aday adōnoy el	מֹשֶׁה אֶת־מוֹעֲדֵי יְיָ אֶל
b'nay yisro-ayl.	בְּנֵי יִשְׂרָאֵל.

These are the set times of the Lord, sacred assemblies, which you shall
proclaim in their appointed seasons. So Moses told the children of Israel
about the set times of the Lord.

For Rosh Hashanah

Tik-u vachōdesh shōfor,
bakeseh l'yōm chagaynu. Ki chōk
l'yisro-ayl hu, mishpot
laylōhay ya-akōv.

תִּקְעוּ בַחֹדֶשׁ שׁוֹפָר,
בַּכֶּסֶה לְיוֹם חַגֵּנוּ. כִּי חֹק
לְיִשְׂרָאֵל הוּא, מִשְׁפָּט
לֵאלֹהֵי יַעֲקֹב.

Blow the shofar in that month, at the full moon, for our festive day. For it is a statute of Israel, an ordinance of the God of Jacob.

Sovray moronon v'rabonon v'rabōsai:

סָבְרֵי מָרָנָן וְרַבָּנָן וְרַבּוֹתַי:

For wine:

Boruch atoh adōnoy,
elōhaynu melech ho-ōlom,
bōray p'ri hagofen.

בָּרוּךְ אַתָּה יְיָ,
אֱלֹהֵינוּ מֶלֶךְ הָעוֹלָם,
בּוֹרֵא פְּרִי הַגָּפֶן.

You are blessed, Lord our God, the sovereign of the world, creator of the fruit of the vine.

For other drinks:

Boruch atoh adōnoy,
elōhaynu melech ho-ōlom,
shehakōl nihyeh bidvorō.

בָּרוּךְ אַתָּה יְיָ,
אֱלֹהֵינוּ מֶלֶךְ הָעוֹלָם,
שֶׁהַכֹּל נִהְיֶה בִּדְבָרוֹ.

You are blessed, Lord our God, the sovereign of the world, by whose word everything came into being.

In the sukkah add:

Boruch atoh adōnoy,
elōhaynu melech ho-ōlom,
asher kid'shonu b'mitzvōsov
v'tzivonu layshayv basukkoh.

בָּרוּךְ אַתָּה יְיָ,
אֱלֹהֵינוּ מֶלֶךְ הָעוֹלָם,
אֲשֶׁר קִדְּשָׁנוּ בְּמִצְוֹתָיו
וְצִוָּנוּ לֵישֵׁב בַּסֻּכָּה.

You are blessed, Lord our God, the sovereign of the world, who made us holy with His commandments and commanded us to live in the sukkah.

זְמִירוֹת לְלֵיל שַׁבָּת
ZEMIRŌS FOR FRIDAY EVENING

1 *Kol m'kadaysh sh'vi-i* כָּל־מְקַדֵּשׁ שְׁבִיעִי

Whoever keeps Shabbos will receive his due reward. Shabbos is a gift from God; it is to be warmly welcomed and enjoyed. May those who observe the laws of Shabbos enjoy God's support.

Kol m'kadaysh sh'vi-i koro-ui	כָּל־מְקַדֵּשׁ שְׁבִיעִי כָּרָאוּי
lō, kol shōmayr shabbos kados	לוֹ, כָּל־שֹׁמֵר שַׁבָּת כַּדָּת
maychal'lō, s'chorō harbayh	מֵחַלְּלוֹ, שְׂכָרוֹ הַרְבֵּה
m'ōd al pi fo-olō, ish	מְאֹד עַל־פִּי פָעֳלוֹ, אִישׁ
al machanayhu v'ish	עַל־מַחֲנֵהוּ וְאִישׁ
al diglō.	עַל־דִּגְלוֹ.
Ōhavay adōnoy ham'chakim l'vinyan	אוֹהֲבֵי יְיָ הַמְחַכִּים לְבִנְיַן
ari-ayl, b'yōm hashabbos	אֲרִיאֵל, בְּיוֹם הַשַּׁבָּת
sisu v'simchu kimkab'lay matan	שִׂישׂוּ וְשִׂמְחוּ כִּמְקַבְּלֵי מַתַּן
nachali-ayl, gam s'u y'daychem	נַחֲלִיאֵל, גַּם שְׂאוּ־יְדֵיכֶם
kōdesh v'imru lo-ayl, boruch	קֹדֶשׁ וְאִמְרוּ לָאֵל, בָּרוּךְ
adōnoy asher nosan m'nuchoh	יְיָ אֲשֶׁר נָתַן מְנוּחָה
l'amō yisro-ayl.	לְעַמּוֹ יִשְׂרָאֵל.
Dōr'shay adōnoy zera avrohom	דּוֹרְשֵׁי יְיָ זֶרַע אַבְרָהָם
ōhavō, ham'acharim lotzays	אֹהֲבוֹ, הַמְאַחֲרִים לָצֵאת
min hashabbos um'maharim	מִן הַשַּׁבָּת וּמְמַהֲרִים
lovō, usmaychim l'shomrō	לָבֹא, וּשְׂמֵחִים לְשָׁמְרוֹ
ul-orayv ayruvō, zeh ha-yōm	וּלְעָרֵב עֵרוּבוֹ, זֶה־הַיּוֹם
osoh adōnoy nogiloh	עָשָׂה יְיָ נָגִילָה
v'nism'choh vō.	וְנִשְׂמְחָה בוֹ.

Zichru tōras mōsheh b'mitzvas	זִכְרוּ תּוֹרַת מֹשֶׁה בְּמִצְוַת
shabbos g'rusoh, charusoh	שַׁבָּת גְּרוּסָה, חֲרוּתָה
la-yōm hash'vi-i k'chaloh bayn	לַיּוֹם הַשְּׁבִיעִי כְּכַלָּה בֵּין
ray-ōseho m'shubotzoh,	רֵעוֹתֶיהָ מְשֻׁבָּצָה,
t'hōrim yiroshuho	טְהוֹרִים יִירָשׁוּהָ
vikad'shuho b'ma-amar kol	וִיקַדְּשׁוּהָ בְּמַאֲמַר כָּל־
asher osoh, vai-chal elōhim	אֲשֶׁר עָשָׂה, וַיְכַל אֱלֹהִים
ba-yōm hash'vi-i m'lachtō	בַּיּוֹם הַשְּׁבִיעִי מְלַאכְתּוֹ
asher osoh.	אֲשֶׁר עָשָׂה.
Yōm kodōsh hu mibō-ō	יוֹם קָדוֹשׁ הוּא מִבֹּאוֹ
v'ad tzaysō, kol zera ya-akōv	וְעַד צֵאתוֹ, כָּל־זֶרַע יַעֲקֹב
y'chab'duhu kidvar hamelech	יְכַבְּדוּהוּ כִּדְבַר הַמֶּלֶךְ
v'dosō, lonu-ach bō v'lismō-ach	וְדָתוֹ, לָנוּחַ בּוֹ וְלִשְׂמֹחַ
b'ta-anug ochōl v'shosō, kol	בְּתַעֲנוּג אָכוֹל וְשָׁתוֹ, כָּל־
adas yisro-ayl yu-usu ōsō.	עֲדַת יִשְׂרָאֵל יַעֲשׂוּ אוֹתוֹ.
M'shōch chasd'cho l'yōd'echo ayl	מְשׁךְ חַסְדְּךָ לְיֹדְעֶיךָ אֵל
kanō v'nōkaym, nōtray yōm	קַנּוֹא וְנֹקֵם, נוֹטְרֵי יוֹם
hash'vi-i zochōr v'shomōr	הַשְּׁבִיעִי זָכוֹר וְשָׁמוֹר
l'hokaym, sam'chaym b'vinyan	לַהֲקֵם, שַׂמְּחֵם בְּבִנְיַן
sholaym uv-ōr ponecho	שָׁלֵם וּבְאוֹר פָּנֶיךָ
tavhikaym, yirv'yun mideshen	תַּבְהִיקֵם, יִרְוְיֻן מִדֶּשֶׁן
baysecho v'nachal adonecho	בֵּיתֶךָ וְנַחַל עֲדָנֶיךָ
sashkaym.	תַשְׁקֵם.
Azōr lashōv'sim bashvi-i	עֲזוֹר לַשּׁוֹבְתִים בַּשְּׁבִיעִי
bechorish uvakotzir	בֶּחָרִישׁ וּבַקָּצִיר
l'ōlomim, pōs'im bō	לְעוֹלָמִים, פּוֹסְעִים בּוֹ
p'si-oh k'tanoh sō-adim bō	פְּסִיעָה קְטַנָּה סוֹעֲדִים בּוֹ
l'voraych sholōsh p'omim,	לְבָרֵךְ שָׁלֹשׁ פְּעָמִים,

tzidkosom tatz-hir k'ōr	צִדְקָתָם תַּצְהִיר כָּאוֹר
shiv-as ha-yomim, adōnoy elōhay	שִׁבְעַת הַיָּמִים, יְיָ אֱלֹהֵי
yisro-ayl hovoh somim, adōnoy	יִשְׂרָאֵל הָבָה תָמִים, יְיָ
elōhay yisro-ayl t'shu-as	אֱלֹהֵי יִשְׂרָאֵל תְּשׁוּעַת
ōlomim.	עוֹלָמִים.

2 M'nuchoh v'simchoh מְנוּחָה וְשִׂמְחָה

By observing Shabbos we acknowledge that the world and all it contains were created by God in six days. Everything is special on Shabbos, from the prayers we recite to the food we eat. Enjoy it—you will be richly rewarded!

M'nuchoh v'simchoh ōr	מְנוּחָה וְשִׂמְחָה אוֹר
la-y'hudim, yōm shabbosōn yōm	לַיְּהוּדִים, יוֹם שַׁבָּתוֹן יוֹם
machamadim, shōm'rov v'zōch'rov	מַחֲמַדִּים, שׁוֹמְרָיו וְזוֹכְרָיו
haymoh m'idim, ki l'shishoh	הֵמָּה מְעִידִים, כִּי לְשִׁשָּׁה
kōl b'ru-im v'ōm'dim.	כֹּל בְּרוּאִים וְעוֹמְדִים.

Sh'may shoma-yim eretz v'yamim,	שְׁמֵי שָׁמַיִם אֶרֶץ וְיַמִּים,
kol tz'vo morōm g'vōhim	כָּל־צְבָא מָרוֹם גְּבֹהִים
v'romim, tanin v'odom v'cha-yas	וְרָמִים, תַּנִּין וְאָדָם וְחַיַּת
r'aymim, ki b'yoh adōnoy tzur	רְאֵמִים, כִּי בְּיָהּ יְיָ צוּר
ōlomim.	עוֹלָמִים.

Hu asher diber l'am	הוּא אֲשֶׁר דִּבֶּר לְעַם
s'gulosō, shomōr l'kad'shō	סְגֻלָּתוֹ, שָׁמוֹר לְקַדְּשׁוֹ
mibō-ō v'ad tzaysō, shabbas	מִבֹּאוֹ וְעַד־צֵאתוֹ, שַׁבָּת
kōdesh yōm chemdosō, ki vō	קֹדֶשׁ יוֹם חֶמְדָּתוֹ, כִּי בוֹ
shovas mikol m'lachtō.	שָׁבַת מִכָּל־מְלַאכְתּוֹ.

B'mitzvas shabbos ayl	בְּמִצְוַת שַׁבָּת אֵל
yachalitzoch, kum k'ro aylov	יַחֲלִיצָךְ, קוּם קְרָא אֵלָיו

yochish l'am'tzoch, nishmas	יָחִישׁ לְאַמְּצָךְ, נִשְׁמַת
kol chai v'gam na-aritzoch, echōl	כָּל־חַי וְגַם נַעֲרִיצָךְ, אֱכֹל
b'simchoh ki k'vor rotzoch.	בְּשִׂמְחָה כִּי כְבָר רָצָךְ.
B'mishneh lechem v'kidush	בְּמִשְׁנֶה לֶחֶם וְקִדּוּשׁ
raboh, b'rōv mat-amim v'ruach	רַבָּה, בְּרֹב מַטְעַמִּים וְרוּחַ
n'divoh, yizku l'rav tuv	נְדִיבָה, יִזְכּוּ לְרַב טוּב
hamis-an'gim boh, b'vi-as	הַמִּתְעַנְּגִים בָּה, בְּבִיאַת
gō-ayl l'cha-yay ho-ōlom habo.	גּוֹאֵל לְחַיֵּי הָעוֹלָם הַבָּא.

3 *Mah y'didus m'nuchosaych*	מַה יְּדִידוּת מְנוּחָתֵךְ

Shabbos Queen! How beloved you are to us. We run to greet you, to kindle the lights and to enjoy all sorts of wonderful delicacies at your three meals. We withdraw from our regular occupations. We should spend special time with our children and take care that the atmosphere should be relaxed and generally delightful. Truly, Shabbos is a taste of the world to come.

Mah y'didus m'nuchosaych, at	מַה־יְּדִידוּת מְנוּחָתֵךְ, אַתְּ
shabbos hamalkoh, b'chayn norutz	שַׁבָּת הַמַּלְכָּה, בְּכֵן נָרוּץ
likrosaych, bō-i chaloh	לִקְרָאתֵךְ, בּוֹאִי כַלָּה
n'suchoh, l'vush bigday	נְסוּכָה, לְבוּשׁ בִּגְדֵי
chamudōs, l'hadlik nayr	חֲמוּדוֹת, לְהַדְלִיק נֵר
bivrochoh, vataychel kol	בִּבְרָכָה, וַתֵּכֶל כָּל־
ho-avōdōs, lō sa-asu	הָעֲבוֹדוֹת, לֹא תַעֲשׂוּ
m'lochoh.	מְלָאכָה.
L'his-anayg b'sa-anugim,	לְהִתְעַנֵּג בְּתַעֲנוּגִים,
barburim uslov v'dogim.	בַּרְבּוּרִים וּשְׂלָו וְדָגִים.
May-erev mazminim, kol minay	מֵעֶרֶב מַזְמִינִים, כָּל־מִינֵי
mat-amim, mib'ōd yōm	מַטְעַמִּים, מִבְּעוֹד יוֹם

muchonim, tarn'gōlim	מוּכָנִים, תַּרְנְגוֹלִים
m'futomim, v'la-arōch kamoh	מְפֻטָּמִים, וְלַעֲרֹךְ כַּמָּה
minim, sh'sōs yaynōs	מִינִים, שְׁתוֹת יֵינוֹת
m'vusomim, v'safnukay	מְבֻשָּׂמִים, וְתַפְנוּקֵי
ma-adanim, b'chol sholōsh	מַעֲדַנִּים, בְּכָל־שָׁלֹשׁ
p'omim.	פְּעָמִים.
L'his-anayg b'sa-anugim,	לְהִתְעַנֵּג בְּתַעֲנוּגִים,
barburim uslov v'dogim.	בַּרְבּוּרִים וּשְׂלָו וְדָגִים.
Nachalas ya-akōv yirosh, b'li	נַחֲלַת יַעֲקֹב יִירָשׁ, בְּלִי־
m'tzorim nachaloh, vichab'duhu	מְצָרִים נַחֲלָה, וִיכַבְּדוּהוּ
oshir vorosh v'sizku	עָשִׁיר וָרָשׁ, וְתִזְכּוּ
lig-uloh, yōm shabbos im	לִגְאֻלָּה, יוֹם שַׁבָּת אִם־
tishmōru, vih-yisem li	תִּשְׁמֹרוּ, וִהְיִיתֶם לִי
s'guloh, shayshes yomim	סְגֻלָּה, שֵׁשֶׁת יָמִים
ta-avōdu, uvash'vi-i nogiloh.	תַּעֲבֹדוּ, וּבַשְּׁבִיעִי נָגִילָה.
L'his-anayg b'sa-anugim,	לְהִתְעַנֵּג בְּתַעֲנוּגִים,
barburim uslov v'dogim.	בַּרְבּוּרִים וּשְׂלָו וְדָגִים.
Chafotzecho asurim, v'gam	חֲפָצֶיךָ אֲסוּרִים, וְגַם
lachashōv cheshbōnōs,	לַחֲשֹׁב חֶשְׁבּוֹנוֹת,
hirhurim mutorim,	הִרְהוּרִים מֻתָּרִים,
ulshadaych habonōs, v'sinōk	וּלְשַׁדֵּךְ הַבָּנוֹת, וְתִינוֹק
l'lam'dō sayfer, lam'natzayach	לְלַמְּדוֹ סֵפֶר, לַמְנַצֵּחַ
binginōs, v'lahagōs	בִּנְגִינוֹת, וְלַהֲגוֹת
b'imray shefer,	בְּאִמְרֵי שֶׁפֶר,
b'chol pinōs umachanōs.	בְּכָל־פִּנּוֹת וּמַחֲנוֹת.
L'his-anayg b'sa-anugim,	לְהִתְעַנֵּג בְּתַעֲנוּגִים,
barburim uslov v'dogim.	בַּרְבּוּרִים וּשְׂלָו וְדָגִים.

Hiluchoch t'hay v'nachas, ōneg	הִלוּכָךְ תְּהֵא בְנַחַת, עֹנֶג
k'ro lashabbos, v'hashaynoh	קְרָא לַשַּׁבָּת, וְהַשֵּׁנָה
m'shubachas, kados nefesh	מְשֻׁבַּחַת, כַּדָּת נֶפֶשׁ
m'shivas, b'chayn nafshi l'cho	מְשִׁיבַת, בְּכֵן נַפְשִׁי לְךָ
or'goh, v'lonu-ach b'chibas,	עָרְגָה, וְלָנוּחַ בְּחִבַּת,
kashōshanim sugoh,	כַּשּׁוֹשַׁנִּים סוּגָה,
bō yonuchu bayn uvas.	בּוֹ יָנוּחוּ בֵּן וּבַת.

L'his-anayg b'sa-anugim,	לְהִתְעַנֵּג בְּתַעֲנוּגִים,
barburim uslov v'dogim.	בַּרְבּוּרִים וּשְׂלָו וְדָגִים.

May-ayn ōlom habo, yōm	מֵעֵין עוֹלָם הַבָּא, יוֹם
shabbos m'nuchoh, kol	שַׁבָּת מְנוּחָה, כָּל־
hamis-an'gim boh, yizku l'rōv	הַמִּתְעַנְּגִים בָּהּ, יִזְכּוּ לְרֹב
simchoh, maychevlay moshiyach	שִׂמְחָה, מֵחֶבְלֵי מָשִׁיחַ
yutzolu lirvochoh, p'dusaynu	יֻצָּלוּ לִרְוָחָה, פְּדוּתֵנוּ
satzmiyach, v'nos yogōn va-anochoh.	תַצְמִיחַ, וְנָס יָגוֹן וַאֲנָחָה.

L'his-anayg b'sa-anugim,	לְהִתְעַנֵּג בְּתַעֲנוּגִים,
barburim uslov v'dogim.	בַּרְבּוּרִים וּשְׂלָו וְדָגִים.

4 Yōm zeh l'yisro-ayl

יוֹם זֶה לְיִשְׂרָאֵל

This is Israel's special day, a day of light, of happiness and of rest, as You commanded us on Mount Sinai. It refreshes us with the gift of an extra soul. You made the world in six days and told us not to work on the seventh day. We know we will be rewarded if we keep Shabbos, but, please God, do not forget that the Temple is still to be rebuilt.

Yōm zeh l'yisro-ayl ōroh	יוֹם זֶה לְיִשְׂרָאֵל אוֹרָה
v'simchoh, shabbas m'nuchoh.	וְשִׂמְחָה, שַׁבַּת מְנוּחָה.

Tziviso pikudim b'ma-amad	צִוִּיתָ פִּקּוּדִים בְּמַעֲמַד
sinai, shabbos umō-adim	סִינַי, שַׁבָּת וּמוֹעֲדִים
lishmōr b'chol shonai, la-arōch	לִשְׁמוֹר בְּכָל־שָׁנַי, לַעֲרוֹךְ
l'fonai, mas-ays va-aruchoh,	לְפָנַי, מַשְׂאֵת וַאֲרוּחָה,
shabbas m'nuchoh.	שַׁבַּת מְנוּחָה.

Yōm zeh l'yisro-ayl ōroh	יוֹם זֶה לְיִשְׂרָאֵל אוֹרָה
v'simchoh, shabbas m'nuchoh.	וְשִׂמְחָה, שַׁבַּת מְנוּחָה.

Chemdas hal'vovōs l'umoh	חֶמְדַּת הַלְּבָבוֹת לְאֻמָּה
sh'vuroh, linfoshōs	שְׁבוּרָה, לִנְפָשׁוֹת
nich-ovōs n'shomoh y'sayroh,	נִכְאָבוֹת נְשָׁמָה יְתֵרָה,
l'nefesh m'tzayroh yosir anochoh,	לְנֶפֶשׁ מְצֵרָה יָסִיר אֲנָחָה,
shabbas m'nuchoh.	שַׁבַּת מְנוּחָה.

Yōm zeh l'yisro-ayl ōroh	יוֹם זֶה לְיִשְׂרָאֵל אוֹרָה
v'simchoh, shabbas m'nuchoh.	וְשִׂמְחָה, שַׁבַּת מְנוּחָה.

Kidashto bayrachto ōsō	קִדַּשְׁתָּ בֵּרַכְתָּ אוֹתוֹ
mikol yomim, b'shayshes kiliso	מִכָּל־יָמִים, בְּשֵׁשֶׁת כִּלִּיתָ
m'leches ōlomim, bō	מְלֶאכֶת עוֹלָמִים, בּוֹ
motz'u agumim hashkayt	מָצְאוּ עֲגוּמִים הַשְׁקֵט
uvit-choh, shabbas m'nuchoh.	וּבִטְחָה, שַׁבַּת מְנוּחָה.

Yōm zeh l'yisro-ayl ōroh	יוֹם זֶה לְיִשְׂרָאֵל אוֹרָה
v'simchoh, shabbas m'nuchoh.	וְשִׂמְחָה, שַׁבַּת מְנוּחָה.

L'isur m'lochoh tzivisonu	לְאִסּוּר מְלָאכָה צִוִּיתָנוּ
nōro, ezkeh hōd m'luchoh	נוֹרָא, אֶזְכֶּה הוֹד מְלוּכָה
im shabbos eshmōroh,	אִם שַׁבָּת אֶשְׁמֹרָה,
akriv shai lamōro minchoh	אַקְרִיב שַׁי לַמּוֹרָא מִנְחָה
merkochoh, shabbas m'nuchoh.	מֶרְקָחָה, שַׁבַּת מְנוּחָה.

Yōm zeh l'yisro-ayl ōroh	יוֹם זֶה לְיִשְׂרָאֵל אוֹרָה
v'simchoh, shabbas m'nuchoh.	וְשִׂמְחָה, שַׁבַּת מְנוּחָה.
Chadaysh mikdoshaynu zochroh	חַדֵּשׁ מִקְדָּשֵׁנוּ זָכְרָה
nechereves, tuv'cho mōshi-aynu	נֶחֱרֶבֶת, טוּבְךָ מוֹשִׁיעֵנוּ
t'noh lane-etzeves, b'shabbos	תְּנָה לַנֶּעֱצֶבֶת, בְּשַׁבָּת
yōsheves bizmir ushvochoh,	יוֹשֶׁבֶת בְּזְמִיר וּשְׁבָחָה,
shabbas m'nuchoh.	שַׁבַּת מְנוּחָה.
Yōm zeh l'yisro-ayl ōroh	יוֹם זֶה לְיִשְׂרָאֵל אוֹרָה
v'simchoh, shabbas m'nuchoh.	וְשִׂמְחָה, שַׁבַּת מְנוּחָה.

5 Yoh ribōn   יָה רִבּוֹן

Lord of all worlds! All Your creatures praise You. Even if we lived a thousand years, we could not recount the extent of Your greatness. God, save Your people from their exile and rebuild the Temple, and there, in Jerusalem, we will really be able to sing to You!

Yoh ribōn olam v'olma-yo,	יָה רִבּוֹן עָלַם וְעָלְמַיָּא,
ant hu malko melech	אַנְתְּ הוּא מַלְכָּא מֶלֶךְ
malcha-yo. Ōvad g'vurtaych	מַלְכַיָּא. עוֹבַד גְּבוּרְתֵּךְ
v'simha-yo, sh'far kodomoch	וְתִמְהַיָּא, שְׁפַר קֳדָמָךְ
l'hachavayoh.	לְהַחֲוָיָה.
Sh'vochin asadayr tzafro	שְׁבָחִין אֲסַדֵּר צַפְרָא
v'ramsho, loch eloho	וְרַמְשָׁא, לָךְ אֱלָהָא
kadisho di v'ro chol	קַדִּישָׁא דִּי בְרָא כָל-
nafsho, irin kadishin	נַפְשָׁא, עִירִין קַדִּישִׁין
uvnay enosho, chayvas boro	וּבְנֵי אֱנָשָׁא, חֵיוַת בָּרָא
v'ōfay sh'ma-yo.	וְעוֹפֵי שְׁמַיָּא.

33

Yoh ribōn olam v'olma-yo,	יָהּ רִבּוֹן עָלַם וְעָלְמַיָּא,
ant hu malko	אַנְתְּ הוּא מַלְכָּא
melech malcha-yo.	מֶלֶךְ מַלְכַיָּא.
Ravr'vin ōvdoych v'sakifin,	רַבְרְבִין עוֹבְדָיךְ וְתַקִּיפִין,
mochaych roma-yo v'zakayf k'fifin,	מָכֵךְ רָמַיָּא וְזָקֵף כְּפִיפִין,
lu yechyay g'var sh'nin	לוּ יֶחֱיֵא גְּבַר שְׁנִין
alfin, lo yay-ōl g'vurtaych	אַלְפִין, לָא יֵעַל גְּבוּרְתֵּךְ
b'chushb'na-yo.	בְּחֻשְׁבְּנַיָּא.
Yoh ribōn olam v'olma-yo,	יָהּ רִבּוֹן עָלַם וְעָלְמַיָּא,
ant hu malko	אַנְתְּ הוּא מַלְכָּא
melech malcha-yo.	מֶלֶךְ מַלְכַיָּא.
Eloho di layh y'kar	אֱלָהָא דִּי לֵהּ יְקָר
urvuso, p'rōk yas onoch	וּרְבוּתָא, פְּרֹק יָת־עָנָךְ
mipum aryovoso, v'apayk yas	מִפֻּם אַרְיָוָתָא, וְאַפֵּק יָת
amoch migō golusa, amoch di	עַמָּךְ מִגּוֹ גָלוּתָא, עַמָּךְ דִּי
v'chart mikol uma-yo.	בְחַרְתְּ מִכָּל־אֻמַּיָּא.
Yoh ribōn olam v'olma-yo,	יָהּ רִבּוֹן עָלַם וְעָלְמַיָּא,
ant hu malko	אַנְתְּ הוּא מַלְכָּא
melech malcha-yo.	מֶלֶךְ מַלְכַיָּא.
L'mikd'shoch tuv ulkōdesh	לְמִקְדָּשָׁךְ תּוּב וּלְקֹדֶשׁ
kudshin, asar di vayh	קֻדְשִׁין, אֲתַר דִּי בֵהּ
yechedun ruchin v'nafshin,	יֶחֱדוּן רוּחִין וְנַפְשִׁין,
vizam'run loch shirin	וִיזַמְּרוּן לָךְ שִׁירִין
v'rachashin, birushlaym karto	וְרַחֲשִׁין, בִּירוּשְׁלֵם קַרְתָּא
d'shufra-yo.	דְשֻׁפְרַיָּא.

Yoh ribōn olam v'olma-yo,	יָהּ רִבּוֹן עָלַם וְעָלְמַיָּא,
ant hu malko	אַנְתְּ הוּא מַלְכָּא
melech malcha-yo.	מֶלֶךְ מַלְכַיָּא.

6 *Tzur mishelō ochalnu* צוּר מִשֶּׁלּוֹ אָכַלְנוּ

My friends, let us bless God whose food we have eaten. He feeds the world and deserves our praise. God, have mercy on us and send the Messiah. Rebuild the Temple and we will sing a new song over a cup brimming with wine.

Tzur mishelō ochalnu, bor'chu	צוּר מִשֶּׁלּוֹ אָכַלְנוּ, בָּרְכוּ
emunai, sova-nu v'hōsarnu,	אֱמוּנַי, שָׂבַעְנוּ וְהוֹתַרְנוּ,
kidvar adōnoy.	כִּדְבַר יְיָ.
Hazon es ōlamō, rō-aynu	הַזָּן אֶת־עוֹלָמוֹ, רוֹעֵנוּ
ovinu, ochalnu es lachmō	אָבִינוּ, אָכַלְנוּ אֶת־לַחְמוֹ,
v'yaynō shosinu, al kayn nōdeh	וְיֵינוֹ שָׁתִינוּ, עַל־כֵּן נוֹדֶה
lishmō, unhal'lō b'finu,	לִשְׁמוֹ, וּנְהַלְּלוֹ בְּפִינוּ,
omarnu v'oninu,	אָמַרְנוּ וְעָנִינוּ,
ayn kodōsh kadōnoy.	אֵין־קָדוֹשׁ כַּיְיָ.
Tzur mishelō ochalnu, bor'chu	צוּר מִשֶּׁלּוֹ אָכַלְנוּ, בָּרְכוּ
emunai, sova-nu v'hōsarnu,	אֱמוּנַי, שָׂבַעְנוּ וְהוֹתַרְנוּ,
kidvar adōnoy.	כִּדְבַר יְיָ.
B'shir v'kōl tōdoh, n'voraych	בְּשִׁיר וְקוֹל תּוֹדָה, נְבָרֵךְ
elōhaynu, al eretz chemdoh,	אֱלֹהֵינוּ, עַל אֶרֶץ חֶמְדָּה,
shehinchil la-avōsaynu, mozōn	שֶׁהִנְחִיל לַאֲבוֹתֵינוּ, מָזוֹן
v'tzaydoh, hisbi-a l'nafshaynu,	וְצֵידָה, הִשְׂבִּיעַ לְנַפְשֵׁנוּ,
chasdō govar olaynu,	חַסְדּוֹ גָּבַר עָלֵינוּ,
ve-emes adōnoy.	וֶאֱמֶת יְיָ.

35

Tzur mishelō ochalnu, bor'chu emunai, sova-nu v'hōsarnu, kidvar adōnoy.

צוּר מִשֶּׁלּוֹ אָכַלְנוּ, בָּרְכוּ אֱמוּנַי, שָׂבַעְנוּ וְהוֹתַרְנוּ, כִּדְבַר יְיָ.

Rachaym b'chasdecho, al am'cho tzuraynu, al tziyōn mishkan k'vōdecho, z'vul bays tif-artaynu, ben dovid avdecho, yovō v'yig-olaynu, ruach apaynu, m'shiyach adōnoy.

רַחֵם בְּחַסְדֶּךָ, עַל עַמְּךָ צוּרֵנוּ, עַל צִיּוֹן מִשְׁכַּן כְּבוֹדֶךָ, זְבוּל בֵּית תִּפְאַרְתֵּנוּ, בֶּן דָּוִד עַבְדֶּךָ, יָבֹא וְיִגְאָלֵנוּ, רוּחַ אַפֵּינוּ, מְשִׁיחַ יְיָ.

Tzur mishelō ochalnu, bor'chu emunai, sova-nu v'hōsarnu, kidvar adōnoy.

צוּר מִשֶּׁלּוֹ אָכַלְנוּ, בָּרְכוּ אֱמוּנַי, שָׂבַעְנוּ וְהוֹתַרְנוּ, כִּדְבַר יְיָ.

Yiboneh hamikdosh, ir tziyōn t'malay, v'shom noshir shir chodosh, uvirnonoh na-aleh, horachamon hanikdosh, yisborach v'yis-aleh, al kōs yayin molay k'virkas adōnoy.

יִבָּנֶה הַמִּקְדָּשׁ, עִיר צִיּוֹן תְּמַלֵּא, וְשָׁם נָשִׁיר שִׁיר חָדָשׁ, וּבִרְנָנָה נַעֲלֶה, הָרַחֲמָן הַנִּקְדָּשׁ, יִתְבָּרַךְ וְיִתְעַלֶּה, עַל־כּוֹס יַיִן מָלֵא כְּבִרְכַּת יְיָ.

Tzur mishelō ochalnu, bor'chu emunai, sova-nu v'hōsarnu, kidvar adōnoy.

צוּר מִשֶּׁלּוֹ אָכַלְנוּ, בָּרְכוּ אֱמוּנַי, שָׂבַעְנוּ וְהוֹתַרְנוּ, כִּדְבַר יְיָ.

זְמִירוֹת לְיוֹם הַשַּׁבָּת
ZEMIRŌS FOR SHABBOS MORNING

7 *Boruch adōnoy yōm yōm* בָּרוּךְ אֲדֹנָי יוֹם יוֹם

We bless the Lord for all He does for His people. Throughout our history—in Egypt, in Babylonia, in Persia and in all the countries of our exile—God has come to save us from the many tyrants who have oppressed us. May God gather us together once more as He promised. Blessed be God who has always been so good to us. Let us extol Him with all our might. May God bless Israel with peace so that we may be able to raise children who will occupy themselves with Torah and the commandments. God is the prince of peace.

Boruch adōnoy yōm yōm,	בָּרוּךְ אֲדֹנָי יוֹם יוֹם,
ya-amos lonu yesha ufidyōm,	יַעֲמָס־לָנוּ יֶשַׁע וּפִדְיוֹם,
uvishmō nogil kol ha-yōm,	וּבִשְׁמוֹ נָגִיל כָּל־הַיּוֹם,
uvishu-osō norim rōsh	וּבִישׁוּעָתוֹ נָרִים רֹאשׁ
elyōn, ki hu mo-ōz ladol	עֶלְיוֹן, כִּי הוּא מָעוֹז לַדָּל
umachseh lo-evyōn. Shivtay	וּמַחְסֶה לָאֶבְיוֹן. שִׁבְטֵי־
yoh l'yisro-ayl aydus,	יָהּ לְיִשְׂרָאֵל עֵדוּת,
b'tzorosom lō tzor b'sivlus	בְּצָרָתָם לוֹ צָר בְּסִבְלוֹת
uv-avdus, b'livnas hasapir	וּבְעַבְדוּת, בְּלִבְנַת הַסַּפִּיר
her-om ōz y'didus, v'nigloh	הֶרְאָם עֹז יְדִידוּת, וְנִגְלָה
l'ha-alōsom may-ōmek bōr	לְהַעֲלוֹתָם מֵעֹמֶק בּוֹר
vodus, ki im adōnoy hachesed	וָדוּת, כִּי־עִם־יְיָ הַחֶסֶד
v'harbayh imō f'dus. Mah	וְהַרְבֵּה עִמּוֹ פְדוּת. מַה־
yokor chasdō b'tzilō l'gōn'naymō,	יָּקָר חַסְדּוֹ בְּצִלּוֹ לְגוֹנְנֵמוֹ,
b'golus bovelōh shulach	בְּגָלוּת בָּבֶלָה שֻׁלַּח
l'ma-anaymō, l'hōrid	לְמַעֲנֵמוֹ, לְהוֹרִיד
borichim nimnoh vaynaymō,	בָּרִיחִים נִמְנָה בֵּינֵמוֹ,
va-yit'naym l'rachamim lifnay	וַיִּתְּנֵם לְרַחֲמִים לִפְנֵי

37

shōvaymō, ki lō yitōsh adōnoy	שׁוֹבֵימוֹ, כִּי לֹא־יִטֹּשׁ יְיָ
es amō, ba-avur hagodōl	אֶת־עַמּוֹ, בַּעֲבוּר הַגָּדוֹל
sh'mō.	שְׁמוֹ.
Aylom shos kis-ō l'hatzil	עֵילָם שָׁת כִּסְאוֹ לְהַצִּיל
y'didov, l'ha-avir mishom	יְדִידָיו, לְהַעֲבִיר מִשָּׁם
mo-uznay mōr'dov, may-avōr	מָאזְנֵי מוֹרְדָיו, מֵעֲבוֹר
bashelach podoh es avodov,	בַּשֶּׁלַח פָּדָה אֶת־עֲבָדָיו,
keren l'amō yorim t'hiloh	קֶרֶן לְעַמּוֹ יָרִים תְּהִלָּה
l'chol chasidov, ki im	לְכָל־חֲסִידָיו, כִּי אִם־
hōgoh v'richam k'rōv chasodov.	הוֹגָה וְרִחַם כְּרֹב חֲסָדָיו.
Utz'fir ho-izim higdil	וּצְפִיר הָעִזִּים הִגְדִּיל
atzumov, v'gam chozus arba	עֲצוּמָיו, וְגַם־חֲזוּת אַרְבַּע
olu limrōmov, uvlibom	עָלוּ לִמְרוֹמָיו, וּבְלִבָּם
dimu l'hashchis es	דִּמּוּ לְהַשְׁחִית אֶת־
r'chumov, al y'day chōhanov	רְחוּמָיו, עַל־יְדֵי כֹהֲנָיו
migayr miskōm'mov, chasday adōnoy	מִגֵּר מִתְקוֹמְמָיו, חַסְדֵי יְיָ
ki lō somnu ki lō cholu	כִּי לֹא־תַמְנוּ כִּי לֹא־כָלוּ
rachamov. Nisgarti le-edōm	רַחֲמָיו. נִסְגַּרְתִּי לֶאֱדוֹם
b'yad ray-ai m'donai, sheb'chol	בְּיַד רֵעַי מְדָנַי, שֶׁבְּכָל־
yōm m'mal'im k'raysom	יוֹם מְמַלְּאִים כְּרֵשָׂם
may-adonai, ezrosō imi	מֵעֲדָנַי, עֶזְרָתוֹ עִמִּי
lismōch es adonai, v'lō	לִסְמֹךְ אֶת־אֲדֹנָי, וְלֹא
n'tashtani kol y'may idonai, ki	נְטַשְׁתַּנִי כָּל־יְמֵי עֲדֹנָי, כִּי
lō yiznach l'ōlam adōnoy.	לֹא יִזְנַח לְעוֹלָם אֲדֹנָי.
B'vō-ō may-edōm chamutz	בְּבוֹאוֹ מֵאֱדוֹם חֲמוּץ
b'godim, zevach lō b'votzroh	בְּגָדִים, זֶבַח לוֹ בְּבָצְרָה
v'tevach lō b'vōg'dim, v'yayz	וְטֶבַח לוֹ בְּבוֹגְדִים, וְיֵז
nitzchom malbushov	נִצְחָם מַלְבּוּשָׁיו

<table>
<tr><td>l'ha-dim, b'chōchō hagodōl</td><td dir="rtl">לְהָאָדִים, בְּכֹחוֹ הַגָּדוֹל</td></tr>
<tr><td>yivtzōr ruach n'gidim, hogoh</td><td dir="rtl">יִבְצֹר רוּחַ נְגִידִים, הָגָה</td></tr>
<tr><td>b'ruchō hakoshoh b'yōm</td><td dir="rtl">בְּרוּחוֹ הַקָּשָׁה בְּיוֹם</td></tr>
<tr><td>kodim. R'ōsō ki chayn</td><td dir="rtl">קָדִים. רְאוֹתוֹ כִּי־כֵן</td></tr>
<tr><td>adōmi ho-ōtzayr, yachshov lō</td><td dir="rtl">אַדְמִי הָעוֹצֵר, יַחְשָׁב־לוֹ</td></tr>
<tr><td>botzroh tiklōt k'vetzer,</td><td dir="rtl">בָּצְרָה תִּקְלֹט כְּבֶצֶר,</td></tr>
<tr><td>umal-och k'odom b'sōchoh</td><td dir="rtl">וּמַלְאָךְ כְּאָדָם בְּתוֹכָה</td></tr>
<tr><td>yinotzayr, umayzid kashōgayg</td><td dir="rtl">יִנָּצֵר, וּמֵזִיד כַּשּׁוֹגֵג</td></tr>
<tr><td>b'miklot yay-otzayr, ehevu</td><td dir="rtl">בְּמִקְלָט יֵעָצֵר, אֲהֵבוּ</td></tr>
<tr><td>es adōnoy kol chasidov</td><td dir="rtl">אֶת־יְיָ כָּל־חֲסִידָיו</td></tr>
<tr><td>emunim nōtzayr. Y'tzaveh tzur</td><td dir="rtl">אֱמוּנִים נוֹצֵר. יְצַוֶּה צוּר</td></tr>
<tr><td>chasdō k'hilōsov l'kabaytz,</td><td dir="rtl">חַסְדּוֹ קְהִלּוֹתָיו לְקַבֵּץ,</td></tr>
<tr><td>may-arba ruchōs odov</td><td dir="rtl">מֵאַרְבַּע רוּחוֹת עָדָיו</td></tr>
<tr><td>l'hikovaytz, uvhar m'rōm</td><td dir="rtl">לְהִקָּבֵץ, וּבְהַר מְרוֹם־</td></tr>
<tr><td>horim ōsonu l'harbaytz,</td><td dir="rtl">הָרִים אוֹתָנוּ לְהַרְבֵּץ,</td></tr>
<tr><td>v'itonu yoshuv nidochim</td><td dir="rtl">וְאִתָּנוּ יָשׁוּב נִדָּחִים</td></tr>
<tr><td>kōvaytz, yoshiv lō ne-emar</td><td dir="rtl">קוֹבֵץ, יָשִׁיב לֹא נֶאֱמַר</td></tr>
<tr><td>ki im v'shov v'kibaytz.</td><td dir="rtl">כִּי־אִם וְשָׁב וְקִבֵּץ.</td></tr>
<tr><td></td><td></td></tr>
<tr><td>Boruch hu elōhaynu asher</td><td dir="rtl">בָּרוּךְ הוּא אֱלֹהֵינוּ אֲשֶׁר</td></tr>
<tr><td>tōv g'molonu, k'rachamov</td><td dir="rtl">טוֹב גְּמָלָנוּ, כְּרַחֲמָיו</td></tr>
<tr><td>uchrōv chasodov higdil lonu,</td><td dir="rtl">וּכְרֹב חֲסָדָיו הִגְדִּיל לָנוּ,</td></tr>
<tr><td>ayleh v'cho-ayleh yōsayf imonu,</td><td dir="rtl">אֵלֶּה וְכָאֵלֶּה יוֹסֵף עִמָּנוּ,</td></tr>
<tr><td>l'hagdil sh'mō hagodōl</td><td dir="rtl">לְהַגְדִּיל שְׁמוֹ הַגָּדוֹל</td></tr>
<tr><td>hagibōr v'hanōro shenikro</td><td dir="rtl">הַגִּבּוֹר וְהַנּוֹרָא שֶׁנִּקְרָא</td></tr>
<tr><td>olaynu. Boruch hu elōhaynu</td><td dir="rtl">עָלֵינוּ. בָּרוּךְ הוּא אֱלֹהֵינוּ</td></tr>
<tr><td>sheb'ro-onu lichvōdō, l'hal'lō</td><td dir="rtl">שֶׁבְּרָאָנוּ לִכְבוֹדוֹ, לְהַלְלוֹ</td></tr>
<tr><td>ulshab'chō ulsapayr hōdō,</td><td dir="rtl">וּלְשַׁבְּחוֹ וּלְסַפֵּר הוֹדוֹ,</td></tr>
<tr><td>mikol ōm govar olaynu</td><td dir="rtl">מִכָּל־אֹם גָּבַר עָלֵינוּ</td></tr>
</table>

chasdō, lochayn b'chol layv	חַסְדּוֹ, לָכֵן בְּכָל־לֵב
uvchol nefesh uvchol m'ōd	וּבְכָל־נֶפֶשׁ וּבְכָל־מְאוֹד
namlichō unyachadō. Shehasholōm	נַמְלִיכוֹ וּנְיַחֲדוֹ. שֶׁהַשָּׁלוֹם
shelō yosim olaynu b'rochoh	שֶׁלּוֹ יָשִׂים עָלֵינוּ בְּרָכָה
v'sholōm, mis'mōl umi-yomin	וְשָׁלוֹם, מִשְּׂמֹאל וּמִיָּמִין
al yisro-ayl sholōm,	עַל־יִשְׂרָאֵל שָׁלוֹם,
horachamon hu y'voraych	הָרַחֲמָן הוּא יְבָרֵךְ
es amō vasholōm, v'yizku	אֶת־עַמּוֹ בַשָּׁלוֹם, וְיִזְכּוּ
lir-ōs bonim	לִרְאוֹת בָּנִים
uvnay vonim ōs'kim	וּבְנֵי בָנִים עוֹסְקִים
batōroh uvmitzvōs,	בַּתּוֹרָה וּבְמִצְוֹת,
al yisro-ayl sholōm,	עַל־יִשְׂרָאֵל שָׁלוֹם,
yō-aytz ayl gibōr avi ad	יוֹעֵץ אֵל גִּבּוֹר אֲבִי־עַד
sar sholōm.	שַׂר־שָׁלוֹם.

8 *Boruch ayl elyōn*   בָּרוּךְ אֵל עֶלְיוֹן

Blessed is God who gives our weary souls rest. God told us to make Shabbos a special day, and we will be amply rewarded for it. Remember to keep Shabbos holy; relax and enjoy its royal feeling. Let the Shabbos Queen bring blessing to your home.

Boruch ayl elyōn asher nosan	בָּרוּךְ אֵל עֶלְיוֹן אֲשֶׁר נָתַן
m'nuchoh, l'nafshaynu fidyōn	מְנוּחָה, לְנַפְשֵׁנוּ פִדְיוֹן
mishays va-anochoh, v'hu	מִשֵּׁאת וַאֲנָחָה, וְהוּא
yidrōsh l'tziyōn ir	יִדְרוֹשׁ לְצִיּוֹן עִיר
hanidochoh, ad onoh tugyōn	הַנִּדָּחָה, עַד אָנָה תּוּגְיוֹן
nefesh ne-enochoh.	נֶפֶשׁ נֶאֱנָחָה.
Hashōmayr shabbos, habayn im	הַשּׁוֹמֵר שַׁבָּת, הַבֵּן עִם
habas, lo-ayl yayrotzu,	הַבַּת, לָאֵל יֵרָצוּ,
k'minchoh al machavas.	כְּמִנְחָה עַל־מַחֲבַת.

40

רוֹכֵב בָּעֲרָבוֹת מֶלֶךְ
עוֹלָמִים, אֶת-עַמּוֹ לְשַׁבֵּת
אִזֵּן בַּנְּעִימִים, בְּמַאֲכָלוֹת
עֲרֵבוֹת בְּמִינֵי מַטְעַמִּים,
בְּמַלְבּוּשֵׁי כָבוֹד
זֶבַח מִשְׁפָּחָה.

הַשּׁוֹמֵר שַׁבָּת, הַבֵּן עִם
הַבַּת, לָאֵל יֵרָצוּ,
כְּמִנְחָה עַל-מַחֲבַת.

וְאַשְׁרֵי כָּל-חוֹכֶה
לְתַשְׁלוּמֵי כֵפֶל, מֵאֵת כֹּל
סוֹכֶה שׁוֹכֵן בָּעֲרָפֶל,
נַחֲלָה לוֹ יִזְכֶּה בָּהָר
וּבַשֵּׁפֶל, נַחֲלָה וּמְנוּחָה
כַּשֶּׁמֶשׁ לוֹ זָרְחָה.

הַשּׁוֹמֵר שַׁבָּת, הַבֵּן עִם
הַבַּת, לָאֵל יֵרָצוּ,
כְּמִנְחָה עַל-מַחֲבַת.

כָּל-שׁוֹמֵר שַׁבָּת כַּדָּת
מֵחַלְּלוֹ, הֵן הֻכְשַׁר חִבַּת
קֹדֶשׁ גּוֹרָלוֹ, וְאִם יֵצֵא
חוֹבַת הַיּוֹם אַשְׁרֵי לוֹ,
לָאֵל אָדוֹן מְחוֹלְלוֹ
מִנְחָה הִיא שְׁלוּחָה.

הַשּׁוֹמֵר שַׁבָּת, הַבֵּן עִם
הַבַּת, לָאֵל יֵרָצוּ,
כְּמִנְחָה עַל-מַחֲבַת.

Rōchayv bo-arovōs melech
ōlomim, es amō lishbōs
izayn ban'imim, b'ma-acholōs
arayvōs b'minay mat-amim,
b'malbushay chovōd
zevach mishpochoh.

Hashōmayr shabbos, habayn im
habas, lo-ayl yayrotzu,
k'minchoh al machavas.

V'ashray kol chōcheh
l'sashlumay chayfel, may-ays kol
sōcheh shōchayn bo-arofel,
nachaloh lo yizkeh bohor
uvashofel, nachaloh umnuchoh
kashemesh lō zor'choh.

Hashōmayr shabbos, habayn im
habas, lo-ayl yayrotzu,
k'minchoh al machavas.

Kol shōmayr shabbos kados
maychal'lō, hayn hachshayr chibas
kōdesh gorolō, v'im yaytzay
chōvas ha-yōm ashray lō,
l'ayl odōn m'chōl'lō
minchoh hi sh'luchoh.

Hashōmayr shabbos, habayn im
habas, lo-ayl yayrotzu,
k'minchoh al machavas.

Chemdas ha-yomim k'ro-ō ayli	חֶמְדַּת הַיָּמִים קָרְאוּ אֵלִי
tzur, v'ashray lismimim	צוּר, וְאַשְׁרֵי לִתְמִימִים
im yihyeh notzur, keser	אִם־יִהְיֶה נָצוּר, כֶּתֶר
hilumim al rōshom	הִלּוּמִים עַל־רֹאשָׁם
yotzur, tzur ho-ōlomim	יָצוּר, צוּר הָעוֹלָמִים
ruchō bom nochoh.	רוּחוֹ בָּם נָחָה.
Hashōmayr shabbos, habayn im	הַשּׁוֹמֵר שַׁבָּת, הַבֵּן עִם
habas, lo-ayl yayrotzu,	הַבַּת, לָאֵל יֵרָצוּ,
k'minchoh al machavas.	כְּמִנְחָה עַל־מַחֲבַת.
Zochōr es yom hashabbos	זָכוֹר אֶת־יוֹם הַשַּׁבָּת
l'kad'shō, karnō ki gov'hoh	לְקַדְּשׁוֹ, קַרְנוֹ כִּי גָבְהָה
nayzer al rōshō, al kayn	נֵזֶר עַל־רֹאשׁוֹ, עַל־כֵּן
yitayn ho-odom l'nafshō, ōneg	יִתֵּן הָאָדָם לְנַפְשׁוֹ, עֹנֶג
v'gam simchoh bohem	וְגַם־שִׂמְחָה בָּהֶם
lō l'moshchoh.	לוֹ לְמָשְׁחָה.
Hashōmayr shabbos, habayn im	הַשּׁוֹמֵר שַׁבָּת, הַבֵּן עִם
habas, lo-ayl yayrotzu,	הַבַּת, לָאֵל יֵרָצוּ,
k'minchoh al machavas.	כְּמִנְחָה עַל־מַחֲבַת.
Kōdesh hi lochem shabbos	קֹדֶשׁ הִיא לָכֶם שַׁבָּת
hamalkoh, el tōch botaychem	הַמַּלְכָּה, אֶל־תּוֹךְ בָּתֵּיכֶם
l'honiyach b'rochoh, b'chol	לְהָנִיחַ בְּרָכָה, בְּכָל־
mōsh'vōsaychem lō sa-asu	מוֹשְׁבוֹתֵיכֶם לֹא תַעֲשׂוּ
m'lochoh, b'naychem	מְלָאכָה, בְּנֵיכֶם
uvnōsaychem eved	וּבְנוֹתֵיכֶם עֶבֶד
v'gam shifchoh.	וְגַם־שִׁפְחָה.
Hashōmayr shabbos, habayn im	הַשּׁוֹמֵר שַׁבָּת, הַבֵּן עִם
habas, lo-ayl yayrotzu,	הַבַּת, לָאֵל יֵרָצוּ,
k'minchoh al machavas.	כְּמִנְחָה עַל־מַחֲבַת.

9   *Yōm zeh m'chubod*   יוֹם זֶה מְכֻבָּד

This is the most precious of days because it is the day on which God rested. You should work for six days, but honor the seventh as Shabbos. Make kiddush, eat challah and other good things. When you are sated, bless God as He has blessed you. The whole universe attests to God's glory and perfection.

Yōm zeh m'chubod mikol yomim,	יוֹם זֶה מְכֻבָּד מִכָּל־יָמִים,
ki vō shovas tzur ōlomim.	כִּי בוֹ שָׁבַת צוּר עוֹלָמִים.
Shayshes yomim ta-aseh	שֵׁשֶׁת יָמִים תַּעֲשֶׂה
m'lachtecho, v'yōm hash'vi-i	מְלַאכְתֶּךָ, וְיוֹם הַשְּׁבִיעִי
laylōhecho, shabbos lō	לֵאלֹהֶיךָ, שַׁבָּת לֹא
sa-aseh vō m'lochoh, ki	תַעֲשֶׂה בוֹ מְלָאכָה, כִּי
chōl osoh shayshes yomim.	כֹל עָשָׂה שֵׁשֶׁת יָמִים.
Yōm zeh m'chubod mikol yomim,	יוֹם זֶה מְכֻבָּד מִכָּל־יָמִים,
ki vō shovas tzur ōlomim.	כִּי בוֹ שָׁבַת צוּר עוֹלָמִים.
Rishōn hu l'mikro-ay	רִאשׁוֹן הוּא לְמִקְרָאֵי
kōdesh, yōm shabbosōn yōm	קֹדֶשׁ, יוֹם שַׁבָּתוֹן יוֹם
shabbos kōdesh, al kayn kol	שַׁבַּת קֹדֶשׁ, עַל כֵּן כָּל־
ish b'yaynō y'kadaysh, al	אִישׁ בְּיֵינוֹ יְקַדֵּשׁ, עַל
sh'tay lechem yivtz'u	שְׁתֵּי לֶחֶם יִבְצְעוּ
s'mimim.	תְמִימִים.
Yōm zeh m'chubod mikol yomim,	יוֹם זֶה מְכֻבָּד מִכָּל־יָמִים,
ki vō shovas tzur ōlomim.	כִּי בוֹ שָׁבַת צוּר עוֹלָמִים.
Echōl mashmanim sh'sayh	אֱכֹל מַשְׁמַנִּים שְׁתֵה
mamtakim, ki ayl yitayn	מַמְתַּקִּים, כִּי אֵל יִתֵּן
l'chōl bō d'vaykim, beged	לְכֹל בּוֹ דְבֵקִים, בֶּגֶד
lilbōsh lechem chukim, bosor	לִלְבּוֹשׁ לֶחֶם חֻקִּים, בָּשָׂר
v'dogim v'chol mat-amim.	וְדָגִים וְכָל־מַטְעַמִּים.

Yōm zeh m'chubod mikol yomim,	יוֹם זֶה מְכֻבָּד מִכָּל־יָמִים,
ki vō shovas tzur ōlomim.	כִּי בוֹ שָׁבַת צוּר עוֹלָמִים.
Lō sechsar kol bō v'ochalto,	לֹא תֶחְסַר כֹּל בּוֹ וְאָכַלְתָּ,
v'sovo-to uvayrachto,	וְשָׂבָעְתָּ וּבֵרַכְתָּ,
es adōnoy elōhecho asher	אֶת־יְיָ אֱלֹהֶיךָ אֲשֶׁר
ohavto, ki vayrach'cho	אָהַבְתָּ, כִּי בֵרֶכְךָ
mikol ho-amim.	מִכָּל־הָעַמִּים.
Yōm zeh m'chubod mikol yomim,	יוֹם זֶה מְכֻבָּד מִכָּל־יָמִים,
ki vō shovas tzur ōlomim.	כִּי בוֹ שָׁבַת צוּר עוֹלָמִים.
Hashoma-yim m'sap'rim k'vōdō,	הַשָּׁמַיִם מְסַפְּרִים כְּבוֹדוֹ,
v'gam ho-oretz mol'oh chasdō,	וְגַם־הָאָרֶץ מָלְאָה חַסְדּוֹ,
r'u ki chol ayleh os'soh	רְאוּ כִּי כָל־אֵלֶּה עָשְׂתָה
yodō, ki hu hatzur	יָדוֹ, כִּי הוּא הַצּוּר
po'olō somim.	פָּעֳלוֹ תָמִים.
Yōm zeh m'chubod mikol yomim,	יוֹם זֶה מְכֻבָּד מִכָּל־יָמִים,
ki vō shovas tzur ōlomim.	כִּי בוֹ שָׁבַת צוּר עוֹלָמִים.

10 *Yōm shabbosōn*   יוֹם שַׁבָּתוֹן

Shabbos is a day of rest which we are all careful to honor. Israel has a covenant with God in which He told us to rest on Shabbos. We will keep our side of the agreement and look to God to keep His to see that no harm befalls us.

Yōm shabbosōn ayn lishkō-ach,	יוֹם שַׁבָּתוֹן אֵין לִשְׁכֹּחַ,
zichrō k'rayach hanichō-ach. Yōnoh	זִכְרוֹ כְּרֵיחַ הַנִּיחֹחַ. יוֹנָה
motz'oh bō monō-ach, v'shom	מָצְאָה בוֹ מָנוֹחַ, וְשָׁם
yonuchu y'gi-ay chō-ach.	יָנוּחוּ יְגִיעֵי כֹחַ.

Ha-yōm nichbod livnay emunim,
z'hirim l'shomrō ovōs
uvonim, chokuk bishnay luchōs
avonim, mayrōv ōnim
v'amitz kō-ach.

הַיּוֹם נִכְבָּד לִבְנֵי אֱמוּנִים,
זְהִירִים לְשָׁמְרוֹ אָבוֹת
וּבָנִים, חָקוּק בִּשְׁנֵי לֻחוֹת
אֲבָנִים, מֵרוֹב אוֹנִים
וְאַמִּיץ כֹּחַ.

Yōnoh motz-oh bō monō-ach,
v'shom yonuchu y'gi-ay chō-ach.

יוֹנָה מָצְאָה בּוֹ מָנוֹחַ,
וְשָׁם יָנוּחוּ יְגִיעֵי כֹחַ.

Uvo-u chulom bivris yachad,
na-aseh v'nishma om'ru
k'echod, ufos'chu v'onu adōnoy
echod, boruch hanōsayn
la-yo-ayf kō-ach.

וּבָאוּ כֻלָּם בִּבְרִית יַחַד,
נַעֲשֶׂה וְנִשְׁמַע אָמְרוּ
כְּאֶחָד, וּפָתְחוּ וְעָנוּ יְיָ
אֶחָד, בָּרוּךְ הַנּוֹתֵן
לַיָּעֵף כֹּחַ.

Yōnoh motz-oh bō monō-ach,
v'shom yonuchu y'gi-ay chō-ach.

יוֹנָה מָצְאָה בּוֹ מָנוֹחַ,
וְשָׁם יָנוּחוּ יְגִיעֵי כֹחַ.

Diber b'kodshō b'har hamōr,
yōm hash'vi-i zochōr
v'shomōr, v'chol pikudov yachad
ligmōr, chazayk mosna-yim
v'amaytz kō-ach.

דִּבֶּר בְּקָדְשׁוֹ בְּהַר הַמֹּר,
יוֹם הַשְּׁבִיעִי זָכוֹר
וְשָׁמוֹר, וְכָל־פִּקּוּדָיו יַחַד
לִגְמוֹר, חַזֵּק מָתְנַיִם
וְאַמֵּץ כֹּחַ.

Yōnoh motz-oh bō monō-ach,
v'shom yonuchu y'gi-ay chō-ach.

יוֹנָה מָצְאָה בּוֹ מָנוֹחַ,
וְשָׁם יָנוּחוּ יְגִיעֵי כֹחַ.

Ho-om asher no katzōn
to-oh, yizkōr l'fokdō b'ris
ushvu-oh, l'val ya-avor bom
mikrayh ro-oh, ka-asher
nishba al may nō-ach.

הָעָם אֲשֶׁר נָע כַּצֹּאן
תָּעָה, יִזְכֹּר לְפָקְדוֹ בְּרִית
וּשְׁבוּעָה, לְבַל יַעֲבָר־בָּם
מִקְרֵה רָעָה, כַּאֲשֶׁר
נִשְׁבַּע עַל־מֵי נֹחַ.

Yōnoh motz-oh bō monō-ach,
v'shom yonuchu y'gi-ay chō-ach.

יוֹנָה מָצְאָה בּוֹ מָנוֹחַ,
וְשָׁם יָנוּחוּ יְגִיעֵי כֹחַ.

11 *Ki eshm'roh shabbos*   כִּי אֶשְׁמְרָה שַׁבָּת

If we observe Shabbos, God will watch over us. It is not a day for pursuing our regular occupation, or even discussing it; rather it is for Torah study. Just as a double portion of mannah fell on Friday, so may God double our portion. We must eat challah; we may not fast on Shabbos except on Yom Kippur. It is a day for good food and good feelings, a day to pray to God in the knowledge that He will answer.

Ki eshm'roh shabbos ayl
yishm'rayni, ōs hi
l'ōl'may ad baynō uvayni.

כִּי אֶשְׁמְרָה שַׁבָּת אֵל
יִשְׁמְרֵנִי, אוֹת הִיא
לְעוֹלְמֵי עַד בֵּינוֹ וּבֵינִי.

Osur m'tzō chayfetz asōs
d'rochim, gam mil'dabayr bō
divray tz'rochim, divray
s'chōroh af divray m'lochim,
ehgeh b'sōras ayl
us-chak'mayni.

אָסוּר מְצֹא חֵפֶץ עֲשׂוֹת
דְּרָכִים, גַּם מִלְדַבֵּר בּוֹ
דִּבְרֵי צְרָכִים, דִּבְרֵי
סְחוֹרָה אַף דִּבְרֵי מְלָכִים,
אֶהְגֶּה בְּתוֹרַת אֵל
וּתְחַכְּמֵנִי.

Ki eshm'roh shabbos ayl
yishm'rayni, ōs hi
l'ōl'may ad baynō uvayni.

כִּי אֶשְׁמְרָה שַׁבָּת אֵל
יִשְׁמְרֵנִי, אוֹת הִיא
לְעוֹלְמֵי עַד בֵּינוֹ וּבֵינִי.

Bō emtzo somid nōfesh
l'nafshi, hinayh l'dōr
rishōn nosan k'dōshi, mōfays
b'says lechem mishneh bashishi,
kochoh v'chol shishi
yachpil m'zō-ni.

בּוֹ אֶמְצָא תָּמִיד נֹפֶשׁ
לְנַפְשִׁי, הִנֵּה לְדוֹר
רִאשׁוֹן נָתַן קְדוֹשִׁי, מוֹפֵת
בְּתֵת לֶחֶם מִשְׁנֶה בַּשִּׁשִּׁי,
כָּכָה בְּכָל שִׁשִּׁי
יַכְפִּיל מְזוֹנִי.

Ki eshm'roh shabbos ayl
yishm'rayni, ōs hi
l'ōl'may ad baynō uvayni.

כִּי אֶשְׁמְרָה שַׁבָּת אֵל
יִשְׁמְרֵנִי, אוֹת הִיא
לְעוֹלְמֵי עַד בֵּינוֹ וּבֵינִי.

<table>
<tr><td>

Rosham b'das ho-ayl chōk el
s'gonov, bō la-arōch lechem
ponim b'fonov, al kayn
l'his-anōs bō al pi
n'vōnov, osur l'vad miyōm
kipur avōni.

</td><td dir="rtl">

רָשַׁם בְּדַת הָאֵל חֹק אֶל־
סְגָנָיו, בּוֹ לַעֲרוֹךְ לֶחֶם
פָּנִים בְּפָנָיו, עַל־כֵּן
לְהִתְעַנּוֹת בּוֹ עַל־פִּי
נְבוֹנָיו, אָסוּר לְבַד מִיּוֹם
כִּפּוּר עֲוֹנִי.

</td></tr>
<tr><td>

Ki eshm'roh shabbos ayl
yishm'rayni, ōs hi
l'ōl'may ad baynō uvayni.

</td><td dir="rtl">

כִּי אֶשְׁמְרָה שַׁבָּת אֵל
יִשְׁמְרֵנִי, אוֹת הִיא
לְעוֹלְמֵי עַד בֵּינוֹ וּבֵינִי.

</td></tr>
<tr><td>

Hu yōm m'chubod hu yōm
ta-anugim, lechem v'ya-yin tōv
bosor v'dogim, hamis-ab'lim
bō ochōr n'sōgim, ki yōm
s'mochōs hu us-sam'chayni.

</td><td dir="rtl">

הוּא יוֹם מְכֻבָּד הוּא יוֹם
תַּעֲנוּגִים, לֶחֶם וְיַיִן טוֹב
בָּשָׂר וְדָגִים, הַמִּתְאַבְּלִים
בּוֹ אָחוֹר נְסוֹגִים, כִּי יוֹם
שְׂמָחוֹת הוּא וּתְשַׂמְּחֵנִי.

</td></tr>
<tr><td>

Ki eshm'roh shabbos ayl
yishm'rayni, ōs hi
l'ōl'may ad baynō uvayni.

</td><td dir="rtl">

כִּי אֶשְׁמְרָה שַׁבָּת אֵל
יִשְׁמְרֵנִי, אוֹת הִיא
לְעוֹלְמֵי עַד בֵּינוֹ וּבֵינִי.

</td></tr>
<tr><td>

Maychayl m'lochoh bō sōfō
l'hachris, al kayn achabes
bō libi k'vōris,
v'espal'loh el ayl
arvis v'shacharis, musof
v'gam minchoh hu ya-anayni.

</td><td dir="rtl">

מֵחֵל מְלָאכָה בּוֹ סוֹפוֹ
לְהַכְרִית, עַל־כֵּן אֲכַבֵּס־
בּוֹ לִבִּי כְּבוֹרִית,
וְאֶתְפַּלְלָה אֶל־אֵל
עַרְבִית וְשַׁחֲרִית, מוּסָף
וְגַם־מִנְחָה הוּא יַעֲנֵנִי.

</td></tr>
<tr><td>

Ki eshm'roh shabbos ayl
yishm'rayni, ōs hi
l'ōl'may ad baynō uvayni.

</td><td dir="rtl">

כִּי אֶשְׁמְרָה שַׁבָּת אֵל
יִשְׁמְרֵנִי, אוֹת הִיא
לְעוֹלְמֵי עַד בֵּינוֹ וּבֵינִי.

</td></tr>
</table>

12 D'ror yikro   דְּרוֹר יִקְרָא

God provides protection for us: praise Him unceasingly and keep Shabbos.
May God restore the Temple and answer the prayer of His people. May He
stamp on our enemies and send the redeemer. May He grant peace to those
who keep Shabbos.

D'ror yikro l'vayn im bas,	דְּרוֹר יִקְרָא לְבֵן עִם בַּת,
v'yintzorchem k'mō vovas,	וְיִנְצָרְכֶם כְּמוֹ בָבַת,
n'im shimchem v'lō yushbas,	נְעִים שִׁמְכֶם וְלֹא יִשְׁבַּת,
sh'vu v'nuchu b'yōm shabbos.	שְׁבוּ וְנוּחוּ בְּיוֹם שַׁבָּת.

D'rōsh novi v'ulomi,	דְּרוֹשׁ נָוִי וְאוּלָמִי,
v'ōs yesha asayh imi,	וְאוֹת יֵשַׁע עֲשֵׂה עִמִּי,
n'ta sōrayk b'sōch karmi,	נְטַע שׂוֹרֵק בְּתוֹךְ כַּרְמִי,
sh'ayh shav-as b'nay ami.	שְׁעֵה שַׁוְעַת בְּנֵי עַמִּי.

D'rōch puroh b'sōch botzroh,	דְּרוֹךְ פּוּרָה בְּתוֹךְ בָּצְרָה,
v'gam bovel asher gov'roh,	וְגַם־בָּבֶל אֲשֶׁר גָּבְרָה,
n'sōtz tzorai b'af v'evroh,	נְתוֹץ צָרַי בְּאַף וְעֶבְרָה,
sh'ma kōli b'yōm ekro.	שְׁמַע קוֹלִי בְּיוֹם אֶקְרָא.

Elōhim tayn b'midbor har,	אֱלֹהִים תֵּן בְּמִדְבָּר הַר,
hadas shitoh b'rōsh tidhor,	הֲדַס שִׁטָּה בְּרוֹשׁ תִּדְהָר,
v'lamazhir v'lanizhor,	וְלַמַּזְהִיר וְלַנִּזְהָר,
sh'lōmim tayn k'may nohor,	שְׁלוֹמִים תֵּן כְּמֵי נָהָר.

Hadōch komai ayl kano,	הֲדוֹךְ קָמַי אֵל קַנָּא,
b'mōg layvov uvam'ginoh,	בְּמוֹג לֵבָב וּבַמְּגִנָּה,
v'narchiv peh unmal'enoh,	וְנַרְחִיב פֶּה וּנְמַלְאֶנָּה,
l'shōnaynu l'cho rinoh.	לְשׁוֹנֵנוּ לְךָ רִנָּה.

48

D'ayh chochmoh l'nafshecho,	דְּעֵה חָכְמָה לְנַפְשֶׁךָ,
v'hi cheser l'rōshecho,	וְהִיא כֶתֶר לְרֹאשֶׁךָ,
n'tzōr mitzvas k'dōshecho,	נְצוֹר מִצְוֹת קְדוֹשֶׁךָ,
sh'mōr shabbos kodshecho.	שְׁמוֹר שַׁבַּת קָדְשֶׁךָ.

זְמִרוֹת לִסְעוּדָה שְׁלִישִׁית
ZEMIRŌS FOR THE THIRD MEAL

13 *B'nay haycholo* בְּנֵי הֵיכָלָא

May the Eternal Holy One join us at Minchah time, when He is especially well-disposed towards us and will show no anger. As He banishes all evil and harmful influences, we will be filled with joy.

Askinu s'udoso	אַתְקִינוּ סְעוּדָתָא
dimhaym'nuso, sh'laymoso	דִּמְהֵימְנוּתָא, שְׁלֵימָתָא
chedvoso d'malko kadisho,	חֶדְוָתָא דְּמַלְכָּא קַדִּישָׁא,
askinu s'udoso d'malko.	אַתְקִינוּ סְעוּדָתָא דְּמַלְכָּא.
Do hi s'udoso diz-ayr	דָּא הִיא סְעוּדָתָא דִּזְעֵיר
anpin v'atiko kadisho	אַנְפִּין וְעַתִּיקָא קַדִּישָׁא
vachakal tapuchin kadishin	וַחֲקַל תַּפּוּחִין קַדִּישִׁין
asyon l'sa-ado bahadayh.	אַתְיָן לְסַעֲדָא בַּהֲדֵהּ.
B'nay haycholo, dichsifin,	בְּנֵי הֵיכָלָא, דִּכְסִיפִין,
l'mechezay ziv diz-ayr anpin.	לְמֶחֱזֵי זִיו דִּזְעֵיר אַנְפִּין.
Y'hōn hocho, b'hai tako,	יְהוֹן הָכָא, בְּהַאי תַּכָּא,
d'vayh malko b'gilufin.	דְּבֵהּ מַלְכָּא בְּגִלּוּפִין.

49

Tz'vu lachado, b'hai va-ado,	צְבוּ לַחֲדָא, בְּהַאי וַעֲדָא,
b'gō irin v'chol gadfin.	בְּגוֹ עִירִין וְכָל־גַּדְפִין.
Chadu hashto, b'hai sha-to,	חֲדוּ הַשְׁתָּא, בְּהַאי שַׁעְתָּא,
d'vayh ra-avo v'lays za-afin.	דְּבֵהּ רַעֲוָא וְלֵית זַעֲפִין.
K'rivu li, chazu chayli,	קְרִיבוּ לִי, חֲזוּ חֵילִי,
d'lays dinin diskifin.	דְּלֵית דִּינִין דִּתְקִיפִין.
L'var natlin, v'lo olin,	לְבַר נַטְלִין, וְלָא עָאלִין,
hanay chalbin dachatzifin.	הֲנֵי כַּלְבִּין דַּחֲצִיפִין.
V'ho azmin, atik yōmin,	וְהָא אַזְמִין, עַתִּיק יוֹמִין,
l'minchoh (l'mitzcho)	לְמִנְחָה (לְמִצְחָא)
aday y'hōn cholfin.	עֲדֵי יְהוֹן חָלְפִין.
R'u dilayh, d'galay layh,	רְעוּ דִילֵהּ, דְּגַלֵי לֵהּ,
l'vatolo b'chol k'lifin.	לְבַטְּלָא בְּכָל־קְלִיפִין.
Y'shavay lōn, b'nōkvayhōn,	יְשַׁוֵּי לוֹן, בְּנוּקְבֵּיהוֹן,
vitam'run b'gō chayfin.	וִיטַמְּרוּן בְּגוֹ כֵפִין.
Aray hashto, b'minchoso,	אֲרֵי הַשְׁתָּא, בְּמִנְחָתָא,
b'chedvoso diz-ayr anpin.	בְּחֶדְוָתָא דִּזְעֵיר אַנְפִּין.

14 Mizmōr l'dovid

מִזְמוֹר לְדָוִד

Mizmōr l'dovid. Adōnoy rō-i, lō	מִזְמוֹר לְדָוִד. יְיָ רֹעִי, לֹא
echsor. Bin-ōs deshe	אֶחְסָר. בִּנְאוֹת דֶּשֶׁא
yarbitzayni, al may m'nuchōs	יַרְבִּיצֵנִי, עַל מֵי מְנוּחוֹת
y'nahalayni. Nafshi y'shōvayv,	יְנַהֲלֵנִי. נַפְשִׁי יְשׁוֹבֵב,
yanchayni v'ma-g'lay tzedek l'ma-an	יַנְחֵנִי בְמַעְגְּלֵי צֶדֶק לְמַעַן
sh'mō. Gam ki aylaych b'gay	שְׁמוֹ. גַּם כִּי אֵלֵךְ בְּגֵיא
tzalmo-ves lō iro ro, ki	צַלְמָוֶת לֹא אִירָא רָע, כִּי
atoh imodi, shivt'cho	אַתָּה עִמָּדִי, שִׁבְטְךָ
umish-antecho, haymoh y'nachamuni.	וּמִשְׁעַנְתֶּךָ, הֵמָּה יְנַחֲמֻנִי.

Ta-ar-ōch l'fonai shulchon, neged	תַּעֲרֹךְ לְפָנַי שֻׁלְחָן, נֶגֶד
tzōr'roy, dishanto vashemen	צֹרְרָי, דִּשַּׁנְתָּ בַשֶּׁמֶן
rōshi, kōsi r'voyoh. Ach	רֹאשִׁי, כּוֹסִי רְוָיָה. אַךְ
tōv vochesed yird'funi	טוֹב וָחֶסֶד יִרְדְּפוּנִי
kol y'may cha-yoy, v'shavti	כָּל-יְמֵי חַיָּי, וְשַׁבְתִּי
b'vays adōnoy l'ōrech yomim.	בְּבֵית יְיָ לְאֹרֶךְ יָמִים.

A psalm of David. The Lord is my shepherd; I shall not want. He makes me lie down in green pastures; He leads me past still waters. He restores my soul; He leads me in the paths of righteousness, for His name's sake. Even though I walk in the valley of the shadow of death, I will fear no evil for You are with me. Your rod and Your staff—they comfort me. You set a table before me in the presence of my enemies. You have scented my head with oil; my cup over-flows. Surely goodness and mercy will follow me all the days of my life and I will dwell in the house of the Lord forever.

15 Y'did nefesh   יְדִיד נֶפֶשׁ

Y'did nefesh ov horachamon	יְדִיד נֶפֶשׁ אָב הָרַחֲמָן
m'shōch avdecho el r'tzōnecho,	מְשׁוֹךְ עַבְדְּךָ אֶל רְצוֹנֶךָ,
yorutz avdecho k'mō a-yol,	יָרוּץ עַבְדְּךָ כְּמוֹ אַיָּל,
yishtachaveh el mul hadorecho,	יִשְׁתַּחֲוֶה אֶל מוּל הֲדָרֶךָ,
ye-erav lō y'didōsecho minōfes	יֶעֱרַב לוֹ יְדִידוֹתֶךָ, מִנֹּפֶת
tzuf v'chol to-am.	צוּף וְכָל-טָעַם.

Hodur no-eh ziv ho-ōlom,	הָדוּר נָאֶה זִיו הָעוֹלָם,
nafshi chōlas ahavosecho,	נַפְשִׁי חוֹלַת אַהֲבָתֶךָ,
ono ayl no r'fo no loh,	אָנָּא אֵל נָא רְפָא נָא לָהּ,
b'har-ōs loh nō-am zivoch,	בְּהַרְאוֹת לָהּ נֹעַם זִיוֶךָ,
oz tis-chazayk v'sisrapay,	אָז תִּתְחַזֵּק וְתִתְרַפֵּא,
v'hoy'soh loh	וְהָיְתָה לָהּ
simchas ōlom.	שִׂמְחַת עוֹלָם.

51

Vosik yehemu no rachamecho,	וָתִיק יֶהֱמוּ נָא רַחֲמֶיךָ,
v'chusoh no al bayn ahuvecho,	וְחוּסָה נָא עַל בֵּן אֲהוּבֶךָ,
ki zeh kamoh nichsōf	כִּי זֶה כַּמָּה נִכְסֹף
nichsafti, lir-ōs	נִכְסַפְתִּי, לִרְאוֹת
b'sif-eres uzecho, ayleh	בְּתִפְאֶרֶת עֻזֶּךָ, אֵלֶּה
chomdoh libi, v'chusoh no	חָמְדָה לִבִּי, וְחוּסָה נָא
v'al tis-alom.	וְאַל תִּתְעַלָּם.
Higoleh no ufrōs chavivi	הִגָּלֵה נָא וּפְרוֹשׂ חֲבִיבִי
olai, es sukkas sh'lōmecho,	עָלַי, אֶת־סֻכַּת שְׁלוֹמֶךָ,
to-ir eretz mik'vōdecho,	תָּאִיר אֶרֶץ מִכְּבוֹדֶךָ,
nogiloh v'nism'choh voch, mahayr	נָגִילָה וְנִשְׂמְחָה בָךְ, מַהֵר
ehōv ki vo mō-ayd,	אֱהוֹב כִּי בָא מוֹעֵד,
v'chonaynu kimay ōlom.	וְחָנֵּנוּ כִּימֵי עוֹלָם.

Beloved of my soul, merciful father, draw Your servant towards You. Let Your servant run as a hind to bow before Your glory. Let Your affection for him be sweeter than a honeycomb or any other delicacy.

Glorious one, most beautiful splendor of the world, my soul is sick with love for You. Please God, heal it by revealing the delight of Your splendor. Then it will be invigorated and healed, enjoying everlasting happiness.

Ancient one, let Your mercy be aroused and have pity on Your beloved son. For I have yearned for so long to see Your mighty splendor. This is the desire of my heart—have pity and do not hide Yourself.

Reveal Yourself and spread over me, beloved one, the shelter of Your peace. Let the earth sparkle with Your glory; we will rejoice and be happy with You. Be quick, beloved, for the time has come, and favor us as in days of old.

הַבְדָּלָה
HAVDOLOH

At the close of Shabbos, Havdoloh is recited over a brimming cup of wine, sweet-smelling spices and a multi-wick candle. At the close of a festival on a weekday evening, omit the first paragraph, the spices and the candle.

Hinayh ayl y'shu-osi, evtach	הִנֵּה אֵל יְשׁוּעָתִי, אֶבְטַח
v'lō efchod, ki ozi	וְלֹא אֶפְחָד, כִּי עָזִּי
v'zimros yoh adōnoy, vai-hi li	וְזִמְרָת יָהּ יְיָ, וַיְהִי לִי
lishu-oh. Ush-avtem ma-yim	לִישׁוּעָה. וּשְׁאַבְתֶּם מַיִם
b'sosōn mima-ai-nay hai-shu-oh.	בְּשָׂשׂוֹן מִמַּעַיְנֵי הַיְשׁוּעָה.
Ladōnoy hai-shu-oh, al am'cho	לַייָ הַיְשׁוּעָה, עַל עַמְּךָ
birchosecho seloh. Adōnoy tz'vo-ōs	בִרְכָתֶךָ סֶּלָה. יְיָ צְבָאוֹת
imonu, misgav lonu elōhay	עִמָּנוּ, מִשְׂגַּב לָנוּ אֱלֹהֵי
ya-akōv seloh. Adōnoy tz'vo-ōs,	יַעֲקֹב סֶלָה. יְיָ צְבָאוֹת,
ashray odom bōtayach boch, adōnoy,	אַשְׁרֵי אָדָם בֹּטֵחַ בָּךְ, יְיָ,
hōshi-oh, hamelech ya-anaynu	הוֹשִׁיעָה, הַמֶּלֶךְ יַעֲנֵנוּ
v'yōm kor-aynu. La-y'hudim	בְיוֹם קָרְאֵנוּ. לַיְּהוּדִים
hoy'soh ōroh v'simchoh,	הָיְתָה אוֹרָה וְשִׂמְחָה,
v'sosōn vikor. Kayn tihyeh	וְשָׂשׂוֹן וִיקָר. כֵּן תִּהְיֶה
lonu. Kōs y'shu-ōs eso,	לָנוּ. כּוֹס יְשׁוּעוֹת אֶשָּׂא,
uvshaym adōnoy ekro.	וּבְשֵׁם יְיָ אֶקְרָא.

Behold God is my salvation, I will have trust and not be afraid. Indeed, the Lord is my strength and my song, and He has become my salvation. You shall draw water with joy from the wells of salvation. Salvation belongs to the Lord; may Your blessings be upon Your people, Selah. The Lord of Hosts is with us, the God of Jacob is a refuge for us, Selah. Lord of Hosts, happy is the man who trusts in You. Lord, save us; may the king answer us on the day we call. ''The Jews had radiance and happiness, joy and honor''—so may it be for us. I will lift up the cup of salvation and call on the name of the Lord.

Sovray moronon v'rabonon v'rabōsai: :סָבְרֵי מָרָנָן וְרַבָּנָן וְרַבּוֹתַי

For the wine:

Boruch atoh adōnoy,	בָּרוּךְ אַתָּה יְיָ,
elōhaynu melech ho-ōlom,	אֱלֹהֵינוּ מֶלֶךְ הָעוֹלָם,
bōray p'ri hagofen.	בּוֹרֵא פְּרִי הַגָּפֶן.

You are blessed, Lord our God, the sovereign of the world, creator of the fruit of the vine.

For the spices:

Boruch atoh adōnoy,	בָּרוּךְ אַתָּה יְיָ,
elōhaynu melech ho-ōlom,	אֱלֹהֵינוּ מֶלֶךְ הָעוֹלָם,
bōray minay v'somim.	בּוֹרֵא מִינֵי בְשָׂמִים.

You are blessed, Lord our God, the sovereign of the world, creator of various kinds of spices.

For the flames:

Boruch atoh adōnoy,	בָּרוּךְ אַתָּה יְיָ,
elōhaynu melech ho-ōlom,	אֱלֹהֵינוּ מֶלֶךְ הָעוֹלָם,
bōray m'ōray ho-aysh.	בּוֹרֵא מְאוֹרֵי הָאֵשׁ.

You are blessed, Lord our God, the sovereign of the world, creator of the lights of fire.

Boruch atoh adōnoy,	בָּרוּךְ אַתָּה יְיָ,
elōhaynu melech ho-ōlom,	אֱלֹהֵינוּ מֶלֶךְ הָעוֹלָם,
hamavdil bayn kōdesh l'chōl,	הַמַּבְדִּיל בֵּין קֹדֶשׁ לְחֹל,
bayn ōr l'chōshech, bayn	בֵּין אוֹר לְחֹשֶׁךְ, בֵּין
yisro-ayl lo-amim, bayn	יִשְׂרָאֵל לָעַמִּים, בֵּין
yōm hash'vi-i l'shayshes	יוֹם הַשְּׁבִיעִי לְשֵׁשֶׁת
y'may hama-aseh.	יְמֵי הַמַּעֲשֶׂה.
Boruch atoh adōnoy,	בָּרוּךְ אַתָּה יְיָ,
hamavdil bayn kōdesh l'chōl.	הַמַּבְדִּיל בֵּין קֹדֶשׁ לְחֹל.

You are blessed, Lord our God, the sovereign of the world, who makes a distinction between sacred and secular, between light and darkness, between Israel and the other nations, between the seventh day and the six working days. You are blessed, Lord, who makes a distinction between the sacred and the secular.

הַמַּבְדִּיל

Hamavdil

Hamavdil bayn kōdesh l'chōl,	הַמַּבְדִּיל בֵּין קֹדֶשׁ לְחֹל,
chatōsaynu hu yimchōl,	חַטֹּאתֵינוּ הוּא יִמְחֹל,
zar-aynu v'chaspaynu yarbeh	זַרְעֵנוּ וְכַסְפֵּנוּ יַרְבֶּה
kachōl, v'chakōchovim baloyloh.	כַחוֹל, וְכַכּוֹכָבִים בַּלָּיְלָה.
Yōm ponoh k'tzayl tōmer,	יוֹם פָּנָה כְּצֵל תֹּמֶר,
ekro lo-ayl olai gōmayr,	אֶקְרָא לָאֵל עָלַי גֹּמֵר,
omar shōmayr, oso vōker,	אָמַר שׁוֹמֵר, אָתָא בֹקֶר,
v'gam loyloh.	וְגַם לָיְלָה.
Tzidkos'cho k'har tovōr,	צִדְקָתְךָ כְּהַר תָּבוֹר,
al chato-ai ovōr ta-avōr,	עַל חֲטָאַי עָבֹר תַּעֲבֹר,
k'yōm esmol ki ya-avōr,	כְּיוֹם אֶתְמוֹל כִּי יַעֲבֹר,
v'ashmuroh valoyloh.	וְאַשְׁמוּרָה בַלָּיְלָה.
Chol'foh ōnas minchosi,	חָלְפָה עוֹנַת מִנְחָתִי,
mi yitayn m'nuchosi,	מִי יִתֵּן מְנוּחָתִי,
yoga-ti v'anchosi,	יָגַעְתִּי בְאַנְחָתִי,
as-cheh v'chol loyloh.	אַשְׂחֶה בְכָל לָיְלָה.
Kōli bal yutal,	קוֹלִי בַּל יֻטַּל,
p'sach li sha-ar ham'nutol,	פְּתַח לִי שַׁעַר הַמְנֻטָּל,
sheroshi nimlo tol,	שֶׁרֹּאשִׁי נִמְלָא טָל,
k'vutzōsai r'sisay loyloh.	קְוֻצּוֹתַי רְסִיסֵי לָיְלָה.
Hay-osayr nōro v'o-yom,	הֵעָתֵר נוֹרָא וְאָיוֹם,
ashavay-a t'noh fidyōm,	אֲשַׁוֵּעַ תְּנָה פִדְיוֹם,

55

b'neshef b'erev yōm,	בִּנְשֶׁף בְּעֶרֶב יוֹם,
b'ishōn loyloh.	בְּאִישׁוֹן לָיְלָה.

K'rosicho yoh hōshi-ayni,	קְרָאתִיךָ יָהּ הוֹשִׁיעֵנִי,
ōrach cha-yim tōdi-ayni,	אֹרַח חַיִּים תּוֹדִיעֵנִי,
midaloh t'vatz'ayni,	מִדַּלָּה תְבַצְּעֵנִי,
miyōm ad loyloh.	מִיּוֹם עַד לָיְלָה.

Tahayr tinuf ma-asai,	טַהֵר טִנּוּף מַעֲשַׂי,
pen yōm'ru mach-isai,	פֶּן יֹאמְרוּ מַכְעִיסַי,
a-yayh elō-ah ōsai,	אַיֵּה אֱלוֹהַּ עֹשָׂי,
hanōsayn z'mirōs baloyloh.	הַנֹּתֵן זְמִרוֹת בַּלָּיְלָה.

Nachnu v'yod'cho kachōmer,	נַחְנוּ בְיָדְךָ כַּחֹמֶר,
s'lach no al kal vochōmer,	סְלַח נָא עַל קַל וָחֹמֶר,
yōm l'yōm yabi-a ōmer,	יוֹם לְיוֹם יַבִּיעַ אֹמֶר,
v'lailoh l'loyloh.	וְלַיְלָה לְלָיְלָה.

He who makes a distinction between the sacred and the secular, may He also pardon our sins. May He proliferate our children and our wealth like the sand, and like the stars at night.

Twilight has arrived like the shade of a palm tree; I call to God who gives me everything. The watchman says morning comes, but night, too.

Your righteousness is as great as Mount Tabor; please ignore, disregard my sins. May they be like yesterday—gone—like a watch in the night.

The time when I would bring offerings is long past. If only I had rest! I am so tired of sighing, I weep every night.

Do not allow my voice to be stifled; open the gate on high for me; for my head is soaked with dew, my locks with the drops of the night.

Grant my prayer, revered and awesome one; I implore You, bring redemption, at dusk, in the evening, in the dark of night.

I am calling You, God, save me; show me life's scheme. Keep me from poverty, by day and by night.

Purify the defilement of my actions, lest those who incite me ask where is the God who made me, who can inspire hymns in the night.

We are as clay in Your hand; please forgive our petty and our major sins. Each day tells the story, and each night.

סדר ברכות

Blessings

בִּרְכַּת הַמָּזוֹן
THE BLESSING AFTER THE MEAL

On Shabbos and Yom Tov, and other occasions of celebration

1 *Shir hama-alōs, b'shuv adōnoy*
es shivas tziyōn ho-yinu
k'chōl'mim. Oz yimolay
s'chōk pinu ulshōnaynu rinoh,
oz yōm'ru vagōyim higdil
adōnoy la-asōs im ayleh.
Higdil adōnoy la-asōs imonu
ho-yinu s'maychim. Shuvoh adōnoy
es sh'visaynu ka-afikim
banegev. Hazōr'im b'dim-oh
b'rinoh yiktzōru. Holōch yaylaych
uvochōh nōsay meshech hazora,
bō yovō v'rinoh nōsay
alumōsov.

שִׁיר הַמַּעֲלוֹת, בְּשׁוּב יְיָ
אֶת־שִׁיבַת צִיּוֹן הָיִינוּ
כְּחֹלְמִים. אָז יִמָּלֵא
שְׂחוֹק פִּינוּ וּלְשׁוֹנֵנוּ רִנָּה,
אָז יֹאמְרוּ בַגּוֹיִם הִגְדִּיל
יְיָ לַעֲשׂוֹת עִם־אֵלֶּה.
הִגְדִּיל יְיָ לַעֲשׂוֹת עִמָּנוּ
הָיִינוּ שְׂמֵחִים. שׁוּבָה יְיָ
אֶת־שְׁבִיתֵנוּ כַּאֲפִיקִים
בַּנֶּגֶב. הַזֹּרְעִים בְּדִמְעָה
בְּרִנָּה יִקְצֹרוּ. הָלוֹךְ יֵלֵךְ
וּבָכֹה נֹשֵׂא מֶשֶׁךְ הַזָּרַע,
בֹּא־יָבֹא בְרִנָּה נֹשֵׂא
אֲלֻמֹּתָיו.

T'hilas adōnoy y'daber pi, vivoraych
kol bosor shaym kodshō
l'ōlom vo-ed. Va-anachnu
n'voraych yoh may-atoh v'ad
ōlom hal'luyoh. Hōdu ladōnoy
ki tōv ki l'ōlom chasdō.
Mi y'malayl g'vurōs adōnoy
yashmi-a kol t'hilosō.

תְּהִלַּת יְיָ יְדַבֶּר פִּי, וִיבָרֵךְ
כָּל־בָּשָׂר שֵׁם קָדְשׁוֹ
לְעוֹלָם וָעֶד. וַאֲנַחְנוּ
נְבָרֵךְ יָהּ מֵעַתָּה וְעַד
עוֹלָם הַלְלוּיָהּ. הוֹדוּ לַיְיָ
כִּי־טוֹב כִּי לְעוֹלָם חַסְדּוֹ.
מִי יְמַלֵּל גְּבוּרוֹת יְיָ
יַשְׁמִיעַ כָּל־תְּהִלָּתוֹ.

A Song of Ascents. When the Lord brought Zion out of captivity, we were like people in a dream. At that time our mouth was filled with laughter and our tongue with cries of joy; at that time it was said among the nations, "The

Lord has done great things for them." The Lord had done great things for us; we were happy. Let our captivity, Lord, be a thing of the past, like dried-up streams in the Negev. Those who sow in tears shall reap in joy. The man who weeps as he trails the seed along will return with cries of joy, carrying his sheaves.

Now let my mouth declare the Lord's praise, and let the whole human race bless His holy name for all time. As for us, we will bless the Lord from now on and forever more: Praise the Lord! Give thanks to the Lord for He is good, for His kindness is everlasting! Who can describe the mighty deeds of the Lord, or utter all His praise?

When three or more men have eaten together, one invites the others to join him in the Blessing after the Meal:

2 *Rabōsai n'voraych.*   רַבּוֹתַי נְבָרֵךְ.

My friends, let us say the blessing.

The others answer

Y'hi shaym adōnoy m'vōroch may-atoh   יְהִי שֵׁם יְיָ מְבֹרָךְ מֵעַתָּה
v'ad ōlom.   וְעַד־עוֹלָם.

May the name of the Lord be blessed from now on and forever more.

The leader repeats

Y'hi shaym adōnoy m'vōroch may-atoh   יְהִי שֵׁם יְיָ מְבֹרָךְ מֵעַתָּה
v'ad ōlom.   וְעַד־עוֹלָם.

May the name of the Lord be blessed from now on and forever more.

and he continues

Birshus   בִּרְשׁוּת

If his father is present he adds

ovi mōri   אָבִי מוֹרִי

If he is a guest at someone else's table he adds

ba-al haba-yis   בַּעַל הַבַּיִת

moronon v'rabonon v'rabōsai n'voraych　　　מָרָנָן וְרַבָּנָן וְרַבּוֹתַי נְבָרֵךְ

If there are ten men present he adds

elōhaynu　　אֱלֹהֵינוּ

she-ochalnu mishelō.　　שֶׁאָכַלְנוּ מִשֶׁלוֹ.

With the consent of (my honored father and) (our host and) all present, let us bless Him (our God) whose food we have eaten.

The others say

Boruch (elōhaynu) she-ochalnu　　בָּרוּךְ (אֱלֹהֵינוּ) שֶׁאָכַלְנוּ
mishelō uvtuvō cho-yinu.　　מִשֶׁלוֹ וּבְטוּבוֹ חָיִינוּ.

Blessed is He (our God) whose food we have eaten and through whose goodness we live.

The leader repeats

Boruch (elōhaynu) she-ochalnu　　בָּרוּךְ (אֱלֹהֵינוּ) שֶׁאָכַלְנוּ
mishelō uvtuvō cho-yinu.　　מִשֶׁלוֹ וּבְטוּבוֹ חָיִינוּ.

Blessed is He (our God) whose food we have eaten and through whose goodness we live.

All say

Boruch hu uvoruch sh'mō.　　בָּרוּךְ הוּא וּבָרוּךְ שְׁמוֹ.

May He be blessed and may His name be blessed.

Individuals begin here:

3　*Boruch atoh adōnoy, elōhaynu*　　בָּרוּךְ אַתָּה יְיָ, אֱלֹהֵינוּ
melech ho-ōlom, hazon es　　מֶלֶךְ הָעוֹלָם, הַזָן אֶת־
ho-ōlom kulō b'tuvō b'chayn　　הָעוֹלָם כֻּלוֹ בְּטוּבוֹ בְּחֵן
b'chesed uvrachamim hu　　בְּחֶסֶד וּבְרַחֲמִים הוּא
nōsayn lechem l'chol bosor, ki　　נוֹתֵן לֶחֶם לְכָל־בָּשָׂר, כִּי
l'ōlom chasdō. Uvtuvō　　לְעוֹלָם חַסְדוֹ. וּבְטוּבוֹ

hagodōl tomid lō chosar	הַגָּדוֹל תָּמִיד לֹא־חָסֵר
lonu v'al yechsar lonu mozōn	לָנוּ וְאַל־יֶחְסַר לָנוּ מָזוֹן
l'ōlom vo-ed. Ba-avur sh'mō	לְעוֹלָם וָעֶד. בַּעֲבוּר שְׁמוֹ
hagodōl ki hu ayl zon	הַגָּדוֹל כִּי הוּא אֵל זָן
umfarnays lakōl umaytiv lakōl	וּמְפַרְנֵס לַכֹּל וּמֵטִיב לַכֹּל
umaychin mozōn l'chōl b'riyōsov	וּמֵכִין מָזוֹן לְכָל־בְּרִיּוֹתָיו
asher boro. Boruch atoh	אֲשֶׁר בָּרָא. בָּרוּךְ אַתָּה
adōnoy, hazon es hakōl.	יְיָ, הַזָּן אֶת־הַכֹּל.

You are blessed, Lord our God, the sovereign of the world, who provides food for the entire world in His goodness, with grace, kindness and mercy; He supplies bread for all living beings, for His kindness is everlasting. Because of His great goodness, we have never lacked food, nor will we ever lack it—on account of His great name—since He is God who feeds and provides for all and is good to all, and who supplies food for all His creatures which He brought into being. You are blessed, Lord, who provides food for all.

4 Nōdeh l'cho adōnoy elōhaynu al	נוֹדֶה לְךָ יְיָ אֱלֹהֵינוּ עַל
shehinchalto la-avōsaynu eretz	שֶׁהִנְחַלְתָּ לַאֲבוֹתֵינוּ אֶרֶץ
chemdoh tōvoh urchovoh,	חֶמְדָּה טוֹבָה וּרְחָבָה,
v'al shehōtzaysonu adōnoy	וְעַל שֶׁהוֹצֵאתָנוּ יְיָ
elōhaynu may-eretz mitzra-yim	אֱלֹהֵינוּ מֵאֶרֶץ מִצְרַיִם
ufdisonu mibays avodim,	וּפְדִיתָנוּ מִבֵּית עֲבָדִים,
v'al b'ris'cho shechosamto	וְעַל בְּרִיתְךָ שֶׁחָתַמְתָּ
bivsoraynu, v'al tōros'cho	בִּבְשָׂרֵנוּ, וְעַל תּוֹרָתְךָ
shelimadtonu, v'al chukecho	שֶׁלִּמַּדְתָּנוּ, וְעַל חֻקֶּיךָ
shehōdatonu, v'al cha-yim chayn	שֶׁחוֹדַעְתָּנוּ, וְעַל חַיִּים חֵן
vochesed shechōnantonu, v'al	וָחֶסֶד שֶׁחוֹנַנְתָּנוּ, וְעַל
achilas mozōn sho-atoh zon	אֲכִילַת מָזוֹן שָׁאַתָּה זָן
umfarnays ōsonu tomid	וּמְפַרְנֵס אוֹתָנוּ תָּמִיד
b'chol yom uvchol ays	בְּכָל־יוֹם וּבְכָל־עֵת
uvchol sho-oh.	וּבְכָל־שָׁעָה.

62

We thank You, Lord our God, for having given the heritage of a lovely, fine and spacious land to our fathers, and for having brought us out, Lord our God, from Egypt, and for rescuing us from slavery, and also for Your covenant which You sealed in our flesh, as well as for Your Torah which You taught us, and Your laws of which You told us, and for the life, grace and kindness You have granted us, and for the food which You supply and provide for us constantly, every day, all the time, and at every hour.

On Chanukah

5 Al hanisim v'al hapurkon	עַל הַנִּסִּים וְעַל הַפֻּרְקָן
v'al hag'vurōs v'al	וְעַל הַגְּבוּרוֹת וְעַל
hat'shu-ōs v'al	הַתְּשׁוּעוֹת וְעַל
hamilchomōs she-osiso	הַמִּלְחָמוֹת שֶׁעָשִׂיתָ
la-avōsaynu ba-yomim hohaym	לַאֲבוֹתֵינוּ בַּיָּמִים הָהֵם
baz'man hazeh.	בַּזְּמַן הַזֶּה.

We thank You for the miracles, for the liberation, for the mighty acts, for the victories, and for the wars which You waged for our ancestors in those days on this occasion.

Bimay matisyohu ben yōchonon	בִּימֵי מַתִּתְיָהוּ בֶּן־יוֹחָנָן
kōhayn godōl chashmōnai uvonov.	כֹּהֵן גָּדוֹל חַשְׁמוֹנַי וּבָנָיו.
K'she-om'doh malchus yovon	כְּשֶׁעָמְדָה מַלְכוּת יָוָן
hor'sho-oh al am'cho yisro-ayl	הָרְשָׁעָה עַל עַמְּךָ יִשְׂרָאֵל
l'hashkichom tōrosecho	לְהַשְׁכִּיחָם תּוֹרָתֶךְ
ulha-avirom maychukay r'tzōnecho.	וּלְהַעֲבִירָם מֵחֻקֵּי רְצוֹנֶךָ.
V'atoh b'rachamecho horabim	וְאַתָּה בְּרַחֲמֶיךָ הָרַבִּים
omadto lohem b'ays tzorosom	עָמַדְתָּ לָהֶם בְּעֵת צָרָתָם
ravto es rivom danto es	רַבְתָּ אֶת־רִיבָם דַּנְתָּ אֶת־
dinom nokamto es nikmosom	דִּינָם נָקַמְתָּ אֶת־נִקְמָתָם
mosarto gibōrim	מָסַרְתָּ גִּבּוֹרִים
b'yad chaloshim v'rabim b'yad	בְּיַד חַלָּשִׁים וְרַבִּים בְּיַד
m'atim utmay-im b'yad	מְעַטִּים וּטְמֵאִים בְּיַד
t'horim ursho-im b'yad	טְהוֹרִים וּרְשָׁעִים בְּיַד

tzadikim v'zaydim b'yad ōs'kay	צַדִּיקִים וְזֵדִים בְּיַד עוֹסְקֵי
sōrosecho. Ulcho osiso shaym	תוֹרָתֶךָ. וּלְךָ עָשִׂיתָ שֵׁם
godōl v'kodōsh b'ōlomecho	גָּדוֹל וְקָדוֹשׁ בְּעוֹלָמֶךָ
ul-am'cho yisro-ayl osiso	וּלְעַמְּךָ יִשְׂרָאֵל עָשִׂיתָ
t'shu-oh g'dōloh ufurkon	תְּשׁוּעָה גְדוֹלָה וּפֻרְקָן
k'ha-yōm hazeh. V'achar kayn	כְּהַיּוֹם הַזֶּה. וְאַחַר כֵּן
bo-u vonecho lidvir baysecho	בָּאוּ בָנֶיךָ לִדְבִיר בֵּיתֶךָ
ufinu es haycholecho v'tiharu	וּפִנּוּ אֶת־הֵיכָלֶךָ וְטִהֲרוּ
es mikdoshecho v'hidliku	אֶת־מִקְדָּשֶׁךָ וְהִדְלִיקוּ
nayrōs b'chatzrōs kodshecho	נֵרוֹת בְּחַצְרוֹת קָדְשֶׁךָ
v'kov'u sh'monas y'may chanukoh	וְקָבְעוּ שְׁמוֹנַת יְמֵי חֲנֻכָּה
aylu l'hōdōs ulhalayl	אֵלּוּ לְהוֹדוֹת וּלְהַלֵּל
l'shimcho hagodōl.	לְשִׁמְךָ הַגָּדוֹל.

It was in the days of Mattathias, son of Yohanan, the High Priest, a Hasmonean, and his sons, that the wicked Hellenistic regime confronted Your people Israel to make them forget Your Torah and to drive them away from the laws of Your will. Then You, in Your great mercy, stood up for them in their time of trouble. You pleaded their cause, argued their case, and avenged their wrong; You delivered the strong into the power of the weak, the many into the power of the few, the impure into the power of the pure, the wicked into the power of the righteous, and the sacreligious into the power of those immersed in Your Torah. Thus You made for Yourself a great and holy name in Your world, and for Your people Israel You brought about a great victory and liberation on this day. And afterwards, Your children came to the sanctuary of Your house, cleared Your holy place, purified Your temple, and kindled lights in Your holy courts, and they established these eight days of Chanukah for giving thanks and praise to Your great name.

On Purim

6 *Al hanisim v'al hapurkon*

v'al hag'vurōs v'al

hat'shu-ōs v'al

עַל הַנִּסִּים וְעַל הַפֻּרְקָן

וְעַל הַגְּבוּרוֹת וְעַל

הַתְּשׁוּעוֹת וְעַל

64

hamilchomōs she-osiso	הַמִּלְחָמוֹת שֶׁעָשִׂיתָ
la-avōsaynu ba-yomim hohaym	לַאֲבוֹתֵינוּ בַּיָּמִים הָהֵם
baz'man hazeh.	בַּזְּמַן הַזֶּה.

We thank You for the miracles, for the liberation, for the mighty acts, for the victories, and for the wars which You waged for our ancestors in those days on this occasion.

Bimay mordechai v'estayr	בִּימֵי מָרְדְּכַי וְאֶסְתֵּר
b'shushan habiroh k'she-omad	בְּשׁוּשַׁן הַבִּירָה כְּשֶׁעָמַד
alayhem homon horosho.	עֲלֵיהֶם הָמָן הָרָשָׁע.
Bikaysh l'hashmid laharōg	בִּקֵּשׁ לְהַשְׁמִיד לַהֲרֹג
ul-abayd es kol ha-y'hudim	וּלְאַבֵּד אֶת־כָּל־הַיְּהוּדִים
mina-ar v'ad zokayn taf v'noshim	מִנַּעַר וְעַד־זָקֵן טַף וְנָשִׁים
b'yōm echod bishlōshoh osor	בְּיוֹם אֶחָד בִּשְׁלֹשָׁה עָשָׂר
l'chōdesh sh'naym osor hu	לְחֹדֶשׁ שְׁנֵים־עָשָׂר הוּא
chōdesh ador ushlolom lovōz.	חֹדֶשׁ אֲדָר וּשְׁלָלָם לָבוֹז.
V'atoh b'rachamecho horabim	וְאַתָּה בְּרַחֲמֶיךָ הָרַבִּים
hayfarto es atzosō	הֵפַרְתָּ אֶת־עֲצָתוֹ
v'kilkalto es machashavtō	וְקִלְקַלְתָּ אֶת־מַחֲשַׁבְתּוֹ
vahashayvōso g'mulō b'rōshō	וַהֲשֵׁבוֹתָ גְּמוּלוֹ בְּרֹאשׁוֹ
v'solu ōsō v'es bonov	וְתָלוּ אוֹתוֹ וְאֶת־בָּנָיו
al ho-aytz.	עַל־הָעֵץ.

It was in the days of Mordecai and Esther, in the capital city of Shushan, that the wicked Haman rose up against them, seeking to wipe out, to murder and to destroy all the Jews, young and old, women and children, on one day, on the thirteenth day of the twelfth month, which is the month of Adar, plundering them for spoil. But you, in Your great mercy, frustrated his plan, and thwarted his intention, and turned the tables on him, so that they hung him and his sons on the gallows.

7 *V'al hakōl adōnoy elōhaynu*   וְעַל הַכֹּל יְיָ אֱלֹהֵינוּ

anachnu mōdim loch   אֲנַחְנוּ מוֹדִים לָךְ

umvor'chim ōsoch yisborach   וּמְבָרְכִים אוֹתָךְ יִתְבָּרַךְ

shimcho b'fi chol chai tomid   שִׁמְךָ בְּפִי כָל־חַי תָּמִיד

l'ōlom vo-ed. Kakosuv   לְעוֹלָם וָעֶד. כַּכָּתוּב,

v'ochalto v'sovo-to uvayrachto   וְאָכַלְתָּ וְשָׂבָעְתָּ וּבֵרַכְתָּ

es adōnoy elōhecho al ho-oretz   אֶת־יְיָ אֱלֹהֶיךָ עַל־הָאָרֶץ

hatōvoh asher nosan loch.   הַטֹּבָה אֲשֶׁר נָתַן־לָךְ.

Boruch atoh adōnoy, al ho-oretz   בָּרוּךְ אַתָּה יְיָ, עַל־הָאָרֶץ

v'al hamozōn.   וְעַל־הַמָּזוֹן.

So for everything, Lord our God, we thank You and bless You—may Your name be blessed in the speech of all living beings, constantly, for all time. For it is written: "And you shall eat, and be satisfied, and bless the Lord Your God for the good land He gave you." You are blessed, Lord, for the land and for the food.

8 *Rachaym adōnoy elōhaynu al*   רַחֵם יְיָ אֱלֹהֵינוּ עַל־

yisro-ayl amecho v'al   יִשְׂרָאֵל עַמֶּךָ וְעַל

y'rushola-yim irecho v'al tziyōn   יְרוּשָׁלַיִם עִירֶךָ וְעַל צִיּוֹן

mishkan k'vōdecho v'al   מִשְׁכַּן כְּבוֹדֶךָ וְעַל

malchus bays dovid m'shichecho   מַלְכוּת בֵּית דָּוִד מְשִׁיחֶךָ

v'al haba-yis hagodōl   וְעַל הַבַּיִת הַגָּדוֹל

v'hakodōsh shenikro shimcho   וְהַקָּדוֹשׁ שֶׁנִּקְרָא שִׁמְךָ

olov. Elōhaynu ovinu r'aynu   עָלָיו. אֱלֹהֵינוּ אָבִינוּ רְעֵנוּ

zunaynu parn'saynu v'chalk'laynu   זוּנֵנוּ פַּרְנְסֵנוּ וְכַלְכְּלֵנוּ

v'harvichaynu v'harvach lonu adōnoy   וְהַרְוִיחֵנוּ וְהַרְוַח־לָנוּ יְיָ

elōhaynu m'hayroh mikol   אֱלֹהֵינוּ מְהֵרָה מִכָּל־

tzorōsaynu. V'no al   צָרוֹתֵינוּ. וְנָא אַל־

tatzrichaynu adōnoy elōhaynu lō   תַּצְרִיכֵנוּ יְיָ אֱלֹהֵינוּ לֹא

liday mat'nas bosor vodom   לִידֵי מַתְּנַת בָּשָׂר וָדָם

v'lō liday halvo-osom, ki	וְלֹא לִידֵי הַלְוָאָתָם, כִּי
im l'yod'cho ham'lay-oh	אִם לְיָדְךָ הַמְּלֵאָה
hap'suchoh hak'dōshoh	הַפְּתוּחָה הַקְּדוֹשָׁה
v'har'chovoh, shelō nayvōsh	וְהָרְחָבָה, שֶׁלֹּא נֵבוֹשׁ
v'lō nikolaym l'ōlom vo-ed.	וְלֹא נִכָּלֵם לְעוֹלָם וָעֶד.

Have mercy, Lord our God, on Israel Your people, on Jerusalem Your city, on Zion the home of Your glory, on the kingdom of the house of David Your anointed one, and on the great and holy house which is called by Your name. Our God, our Father—look after us and feed us, give us a livelihood and support us, and provide a respite for us—a respite for us, Lord our God, soon, from all our troubles. And please, let us not be dependent, Lord our God, neither on a gift, nor on a loan from a human being, but rather on Your full, open, holy and generous hand, so that we should never feel embarrassed or ashamed.

On Shabbos

9

R'tzayh v'hachalitzaynu adōnoy	רְצֵה וְהַחֲלִיצֵנוּ יְיָ
elōhaynu b'mitzvōsecho	אֱלֹהֵינוּ בְּמִצְוֹתֶיךָ
uvmitzvas yōm hash'vi-i	וּבְמִצְוַת יוֹם הַשְּׁבִיעִי
hashabbos hagodōl v'hakodōsh	הַשַּׁבָּת הַגָּדוֹל וְהַקָּדוֹשׁ
hazeh. Ki yōm zeh godōl	הַזֶּה. כִּי יוֹם זֶה גָּדוֹל
v'kodōsh hu l'fonecho	וְקָדוֹשׁ הוּא לְפָנֶיךָ
lishbōs bō v'lonu-ach bō	לִשְׁבָּת־בּוֹ וְלָנוּחַ בּוֹ
b'ahavoh k'mitzvas r'tzōnecho.	בְּאַהֲבָה כְּמִצְוַת רְצוֹנֶךָ.
Uvirtzōn'cho honiyach lonu adōnoy	וּבִרְצוֹנְךָ הָנִיחַ לָנוּ יְיָ
elōhaynu shelō s'hay tzoroh	אֱלֹהֵינוּ שֶׁלֹּא תְהֵא צָרָה
v'yogōn va-anochoh b'yōm	וְיָגוֹן וַאֲנָחָה בְּיוֹם
m'nuchosaynu. V'har-aynu adōnoy	מְנוּחָתֵנוּ. וְהַרְאֵנוּ יְיָ
elōhaynu b'nechomas tziyōn	אֱלֹהֵינוּ בְּנֶחָמַת צִיּוֹן
irecho uv'vinyan y'rushola-yim	עִירֶךָ וּבְבִנְיַן יְרוּשָׁלַיִם
ir kodshecho ki atoh hu	עִיר קָדְשֶׁךָ כִּי אַתָּה הוּא

ba-al ha-yshu-ōs uva-al
hanechomōs.

בַּעַל הַיְשׁוּעוֹת וּבַעַל
הַנֶּחָמוֹת.

Be pleased, Lord our God, to strengthen us through Your commandments, especially the commandment of the seventh day, this great and holy Shabbos. For this is indeed a great and holy day for You; to rest and to be at ease, with loving concern for the command of Your will. So may it please You to grant us rest, Lord our God, with no trouble, or unhappiness, or weeping on our day of rest. And let us witness, Lord our God, the consolation of Zion, Your city, and the building up of Jerusalem, Your holy city, for You are the Lord of redemption, and the Lord of consolation.

On Rosh Chodesh and Yom Tov

10 Elōhaynu vaylōhay avōsaynu,
ya-aleh v'yovō v'yagi-a v'yayro-eh
v'yayrotzeh v'yishoma v'yipokayd
v'yizochayr zichrōnaynu ufikdōnaynu,
v'zichrōn avōsaynu, v'zichrōn
moshiyach ben dovid avdecho,
v'zichrōn y'rushola-yim ir
kodshecho, v'zichrōn kol am'cho
bays yisro-ayl l'fonecho,
liflaytoh ultōvoh ulchayn
ulchesed ulrachamim ulcha-yim
ulsholōm b'yōm

אֱלֹהֵינוּ וֵאלֹהֵי אֲבוֹתֵינוּ,
יַעֲלֶה וְיָבֹא וְיַגִּיעַ וְיֵרָאֶה
וְיֵרָצֶה וְיִשָּׁמַע וְיִפָּקֵד
וְיִזָּכֵר זִכְרוֹנֵנוּ וּפִקְדוֹנֵנוּ,
וְזִכְרוֹן אֲבוֹתֵינוּ, וְזִכְרוֹן
מָשִׁיחַ בֶּן־דָּוִד עַבְדֶּךָ,
וְזִכְרוֹן יְרוּשָׁלַיִם עִיר
קָדְשֶׁךָ, וְזִכְרוֹן כָּל־עַמְּךָ
בֵּית יִשְׂרָאֵל לְפָנֶיךָ,
לִפְלֵיטָה לְטוֹבָה לְחֵן
וּלְחֶסֶד וּלְרַחֲמִים לְחַיִּים
וּלְשָׁלוֹם בְּיוֹם

Rosh Chodesh

rōsh hachōdesh hazeh.

רֹאשׁ הַחֹדֶשׁ הַזֶּה.

Rosh Hashanah

hazikorōn hazeh.

הַזִּכָּרוֹן הַזֶּה.

Sukkos

chag hasukkos hazeh.

חַג הַסֻּכּוֹת הַזֶּה.

Sh'mini Atzeres and Simchas Torah

hash'mini chag ho-atzeres
hazeh.

הַשְּׁמִינִי חַג הָעֲצֶרֶת
הַזֶּה.

Pesach

chag hamatzōs hazeh.

חַג הַמַּצּוֹת הַזֶּה.

Shavuos

chag hashovu-ōs hazeh.

חַג הַשָּׁבֻעוֹת הַזֶּה.

Zochraynu adōnoy elōhaynu bō
l'tōvoh ufokdaynu vō
livrochoh v'hōshi-aynu vō
l'cha-yim. Uvidvar y'shu-oh
v'rachamim chus v'chonaynu v'rachaym
olaynu v'hōshi-aynu, ki
aylecho aynaynu, ki ayl melech
chanun v'rachum otoh.

זָכְרֵנוּ יְיָ אֱלֹהֵינוּ בּוֹ
לְטוֹבָה וּפָקְדֵנוּ בוֹ
לִבְרָכָה וְהוֹשִׁיעֵנוּ בוֹ
לְחַיִּים. וּבִדְבַר יְשׁוּעָה
וְרַחֲמִים חוּס וְחָנֵּנוּ וְרַחֵם
עָלֵינוּ וְהוֹשִׁיעֵנוּ, כִּי
אֵלֶיךָ עֵינֵינוּ, כִּי אֵל מֶלֶךְ
חַנּוּן וְרַחוּם אָתָּה.

Our God and God of our fathers, may a reminder and a remembrance of us, and of our fathers, and of the Messiah the son of David Your servant, and of Jerusalem Your holy city, and of all Your people the house of Israel, ascend and arrive, reach and be noticed, and accepted, heard, noted and remembered before You, for deliverance and well-being, for grace, kindness and mercy, for life and peace—on this day of

the New Month/Remembrance/the Festival of Sukkot/the Eighth Day of Assembly Festival/the Festival of Unleavened Bread/the Festival of Shavuos.

Be mindful of us, Lord our God, on this day, for good, take note of us for blessing and preserve us in life. And with an act of redemption and mercy, have pity on us and be gracious to us, and be merciful to us and save us, for our eyes are directed toward You, for You are a gracious and merciful divine ruler.

11   *Uvnayh y'rushola-yim ir*   וּבְנֵה יְרוּשָׁלַיִם עִיר

hakōdesh bimhayroh v'yomaynu.   הַקֹּדֶשׁ בִּמְהֵרָה בְיָמֵינוּ.

Boruch atoh adōnoy, bōneh   בָּרוּךְ אַתָּה יְיָ, בּוֹנֵה

v'rachamov y'rusholo-yim. Omayn.   בְּרַחֲמָיו יְרוּשָׁלָיִם. אָמֵן.

And may You build up Jerusalem, the holy city, rapidly in our lifetimes.
You are blessed, Lord, who in His mercy, builds up Jerusalem. Amen.

12   *Boruch atoh adōnoy, elōhaynu*   בָּרוּךְ אַתָּה יְיָ, אֱלֹהֵינוּ

melech ho-ōlom, ho-ayl ovinu   מֶלֶךְ הָעוֹלָם, הָאֵל אָבִינוּ

malkaynu adiraynu bōr'aynu   מַלְכֵּנוּ אַדִּירֵנוּ בּוֹרְאֵנוּ

gō-alaynu yōtz'raynu k'dōshaynu   גּוֹאֲלֵנוּ יוֹצְרֵנוּ קְדוֹשֵׁנוּ

k'dōsh ya-akōv, rō-aynu rō-ayh   קְדוֹשׁ יַעֲקֹב, רוֹעֵנוּ רוֹעֵה

yisro-ayl hamelech hatōv   יִשְׂרָאֵל הַמֶּלֶךְ הַטּוֹב

v'hamaytiv lakōl sheb'chol yōm   וְהַמֵּטִיב לַכֹּל שֶׁבְּכָל־יוֹם

vo-yōm hu haytiv hu   וָיוֹם הוּא הֵטִיב הוּא

maytiv hu yaytiv lonu.   מֵטִיב הוּא יֵיטִיב לָנוּ.

Hu g'molonu hu gōm'laynu   הוּא גְמָלָנוּ הוּא גוֹמְלֵנוּ

hu yigm'laynu lo-ad l'chayn   הוּא יִגְמְלֵנוּ לָעַד לְחֵן

l'chesed ulrachamim ulrevach   לְחֶסֶד וּלְרַחֲמִים וּלְרֶוַח

hatzoloh v'hatzlochoh b'rochoh   הַצָּלָה וְהַצְלָחָה בְּרָכָה

vishu-oh nechomoh parnosoh   וִישׁוּעָה נֶחָמָה פַּרְנָסָה

v'chalkoloh v'rachamim v'cha-yim   וְכַלְכָּלָה וְרַחֲמִים וְחַיִּים

v'sholōm v'chol tōv, umikol   וְשָׁלוֹם וְכָל־טוֹב, וּמִכָּל־

tōv l'ōlom al y'chas'raynu.   טוֹב לְעוֹלָם אַל־יְחַסְּרֵנוּ.

You are blessed, Lord our God, the sovereign of the world—God who is
our father, our king, our mighty one, our creator, our redeemer, our maker,
our holy one—the holy one of Jacob; our shepherd—the shepherd of Israel;
the king who is good and who does good to all, who each and every day has
been good, is good and will be good to us. He gave, gives, and will always give
us grace, kindness and mercy, and respite, deliverance and success, blessing

and salvation, comfort, a livelihood and sustenance, and mercy and life and peace and everything that is good—and may He never let us lack anything that is good.

13

Horachamon hu yimlōch olaynu	הָרַחֲמָן הוּא יִמְלוֹךְ עָלֵינוּ
l'ōlom vo-ed. Horachamon hu	לְעוֹלָם וָעֶד. הָרַחֲמָן הוּא
yisborach bashoma-yim uvo-oretz.	יִתְבָּרַךְ בַּשָּׁמַיִם וּבָאָרֶץ.
Horachamon hu yishtabach	הָרַחֲמָן הוּא יִשְׁתַּבַּח
l'dōr dōrim v'yispo-ar bonu	לְדוֹר דּוֹרִים וְיִתְפָּאַר בָּנוּ
l'naytzach n'tzochim v'yis-hadar	לָנֵצַח נְצָחִים וְיִתְהַדַּר
bonu lo-ad ul-ōl'may	בָּנוּ לָעַד וּלְעוֹלְמֵי
ōlomim. Horachamon hu	עוֹלָמִים. הָרַחֲמָן הוּא
y'farn'saynu b'chovōd. Horachamon	יְפַרְנְסֵנוּ בְּכָבוֹד. הָרַחֲמָן
hu yishbōr ulaynu may-al	הוּא יִשְׁבּוֹר עֻלֵנוּ מֵעַל
tzavoraynu v'hu yōlichaynu	צַוָּארֵנוּ וְהוּא יוֹלִיכֵנוּ
kōm'mi-us l'artzaynu.	קוֹמְמִיּוּת לְאַרְצֵנוּ.
Horachamon hu yishlach	הָרַחֲמָן הוּא יִשְׁלַח
b'rochoh m'ruboh baba-yis hazeh	בְּרָכָה מְרֻבָּה בַּבַּיִת הַזֶּה
v'al shulchon zeh she-ochalnu	וְעַל שֻׁלְחָן זֶה שֶׁאָכַלְנוּ
olov. Horachamon hu yishlach	עָלָיו. הָרַחֲמָן הוּא יִשְׁלַח
lonu es ayliyohu hanovi	לָנוּ אֶת־אֵלִיָּהוּ הַנָּבִיא
zochur latōv vivaser lonu	זָכוּר לַטּוֹב וִיבַשֶּׂר־לָנוּ
b'sōrōs tōvōs y'shu-ōs	בְּשׂוֹרוֹת טוֹבוֹת יְשׁוּעוֹת
v'nechomōs.	וְנֶחָמוֹת.

The Merciful One—He will rule over us forever. May the Merciful One he blessed in heaven and on earth. May the Merciful One be praised for generation upon generation, and may He be glorified through us forever and ever, and may He be honored through us eternally. May the Merciful One grant us an honorable livelihood. May the Merciful One break the yoke from our neck and lead us upright to our land. May the Merciful One send a plentiful blessing on this house and on this table at which we have eaten. May the Merciful One send us Elijah the prophet—who is remembered for good— who will bring us good tidings of salvation and comfort.

14 *Y'hi rotzōn shelō yayvōsh*

יְהִי רָצוֹן שֶׁלֹּא יֵבוֹשׁ

v'lō yikolaym ba-al haba-yis

וְלֹא יִכָּלֵם בַּעַל הַבַּיִת

hazeh, lō vo-ōlom hazeh v'lō

הַזֶּה, לֹא בָעוֹלָם הַזֶּה וְלֹא

vo-ōlom habo. V'yatzli-ach

בָעוֹלָם הַבָּא, וְיַצְלִיחַ

bechol nechosov, v'yihyu

בְּכָל נְכָסָיו, וְיִהְיוּ

nechosov mutzlochim ukrōvim

נְכָסָיו מוּצְלָחִים וּקְרוֹבִים

lo-ir, v'al yishlōt soton

לָעִיר, וְאַל יִשְׁלוֹט שָׂטָן

b'ma-asay yodov, v'al

בְּמַעֲשֵׂה יָדָיו, וְאַל

yizdakek lefonov shum d'var

יִזְדַּקֵּק לְפָנָיו שׁוּם דְּבַר

chet v'hirhur ovōn, may-atoh

חֵטְא וְהִרְהוּר עָוֹן, מֵעַתָּה

v'ad ōlom.

וְעַד עוֹלָם.

May it be Your will that the master of this house should never be feel embarrassed or ashamed, neither in this world nor in the world-to-come. May he prosper in all he undertakes; may his endeavors be successful and close to home; may no evil force hold sway over his efforts; let not even any suggestion of wrongdoing or sinful idea attach itself to him, from now on and forever.

**These personal blessings are added according to
the individual circumstances**

15 *Horachamon hu y'voraych*

הָרַחֲמָן הוּא יְבָרֵךְ

May the Merciful One bless

for one's parents

es ovi mōri (ba-al

אֶת־אָבִי מוֹרִי (בַּעַל

haba-yis hazeh) v'es imi

הַבַּיִת הַזֶּה) וְאֶת־אִמִּי

mōrosi (ba-alas haba-yis

מוֹרָתִי (בַּעֲלַת הַבַּיִת

hazeh), ōsom v'es baysom

הַזֶּה), אוֹתָם וְאֶת־בֵּיתָם

v'es zar-om v'es kol

וְאֶת־זַרְעָם וְאֶת־כָּל־

asher lohem,

אֲשֶׁר לָהֶם,

my honored father (the man of this house) and my honored mother (the woman of this house) them, together with their household, their children and everything that is theirs.

for oneself and one's own family

ōsi v'es ishti (ba-ali)

אוֹתִי וְאֶת־אִשְׁתִּי (בַּעֲלִי)

v'es zar-i v'es kol asher li,

וְאֶת־זַרְעִי וְאֶת־כָּל־אֲשֶׁר לִי,

me, my wife (my husband), together with everything that is mine,

for one's hosts

es ba-al haba-yis hazeh

אֶת־בַּעַל הַבַּיִת הַזֶּה

v'es ba-alas haba-yis hazeh,

וְאֶת־בַּעֲלַת הַבַּיִת הַזֶּה,

ōsom v'es baysom v'es

אוֹתָם וְאֶת־בֵּיתָם וְאֶת־

zar-om v'es kol asher lohem,

זַרְעָם וְאֶת־כָּל־אֲשֶׁר לָהֶם,

the man of this house and the woman of this house—them, together with their household, their children and everything that is theirs,

for others present

v'es kol ham'subin kon,

וְאֶת־כָּל־הַמְסֻבִּין כָּאן,

and all those who are seated here,

—ōsonu v'es kol asher

— אוֹתָנוּ וְאֶת־כָּל־אֲשֶׁר

lonu, k'mō shenisbor'chu

לָנוּ, כְּמוֹ שֶׁנִּתְבָּרְכוּ

avōsaynu avrohom yitzchok

אֲבוֹתֵינוּ אַבְרָהָם יִצְחָק

v'ya-akōv bakōl mikōl kōl, kayn

וְיַעֲקֹב בַּכֹּל מִכֹּל כֹּל, כֵּן

y'voraych ōsonu kulonu yachad

יְבָרֵךְ אוֹתָנוּ כֻּלָּנוּ יַחַד

bivrochoh sh'laymoh, v'nōmar

בִּבְרָכָה שְׁלֵמָה, וְנֹאמַר

omayn.

אָמֵן.

—us, together with all that is ours, just as our fathers, Abraham, Isaac and Jacob, were blessed—totally—so may He bless us, all of us together, with a complete blessing, and let us say, Amen.

16 *Bamorōm y'lam'du alayhem* בַּמָּרוֹם יְלַמְּדוּ עֲלֵיהֶם

v'olaynu z'chus shet'hay וְעָלֵינוּ זְכוּת שֶׁתְּהֵא

l'mishmeres sholōm. V'niso לְמִשְׁמֶרֶת שָׁלוֹם. וְנִשָּׂא

v'rochoh may-ays adōnoy utzdokoh בְרָכָה מֵאֵת יְיָ וּצְדָקָה

may-elōhay yish-aynu. V'nimtzo מֵאֱלֹהֵי יִשְׁעֵנוּ. וְנִמְצָא־

chayn v'saychel tōv b'aynay חֵן וְשֵׂכֶל טוֹב בְּעֵינֵי

elōhim v'odom. אֱלֹהִים וְאָדָם.

May a plea be heard on high, for them and for us, which will result in the security of peace. So may we receive a blessing from the Lord and righteousness from the God of our salvation. So may we find favor and understanding in the sight of God and man.

On Shabbos

17 *Horachamon hu yanchilaynu* הָרַחֲמָן הוּא יַנְחִילֵנוּ

yōm shekulō shabbos umnuchoh יוֹם שֶׁכֻּלּוֹ שַׁבָּת וּמְנוּחָה

l'cha-yay ho-ōlomim. לְחַיֵּי הָעוֹלָמִים.

May the Merciful One bring us the day which will be totally Shabbos and rest, in everlasting life.

On Rosh Chodesh

Horachamon hu y'chadaysh olaynu הָרַחֲמָן הוּא יְחַדֵּשׁ עָלֵינוּ

es hachōdesh hazeh l'tōvoh אֶת־הַחֹדֶשׁ הַזֶּה לְטוֹבָה

v'livro-choh. וְלִבְרָכָה.

May the Merciful One introduce this month to us with goodness and blessing.

On Yom Tov

Horachamon hu yanchilaynu yōm הָרַחֲמָן הוּא יַנְחִילֵנוּ יוֹם

shekulō tōv. שֶׁכֻּלּוֹ טוֹב.

May the Merciful One bring us the day which will be totally good.

On Rosh Hashanah

Horachamon hu y'chadaysh olaynu
es hashonoh hazos l'tōvoh
v'livrochoh.

הָרַחֲמָן הוּא יְחַדֵּשׁ עָלֵינוּ
אֶת־הַשָּׁנָה הַזֹּאת לְטוֹבָה
וְלִבְרָכָה.

May the Merciful One introduce this year to us with goodness and blessing.

On Sukkos

Horachamon hu yokim lonu
es sukkas dovid hanōfeles.

הָרַחֲמָן הוּא יָקִים לָנוּ
אֶת־סֻכַּת דָּוִד הַנּוֹפֶלֶת.

May the Merciful One raise up for us the fallen sukkah of David.

On other days, continue here

18 *Horachamon hu y'zakaynu limōs*
hamoshiyach ulcha-yay ho-ōlom
habo.

הָרַחֲמָן הוּא יְזַכֵּנוּ לִימוֹת
הַמָּשִׁיחַ וּלְחַיֵּי הָעוֹלָם
הַבָּא.

May the Merciful One make us worthy of experiencing the days of the Messiah and the life of the world to come.

On Shabbos, Yom Tov and Rosh Chodesh
Migdōl

מִגְדּוֹל

On other days
Magdil

מַגְדִּיל

y'shu-ōs malkō v'ōseh
chesed limshichō l'dovid
ulzar-ō ad ōlom. Ōseh
sholōm bimrōmov hu
ya-aseh sholōm olaynu v'al
kol yisro-ayl, v'imru omayn.

יְשׁוּעוֹת מַלְכּוֹ וְעֹשֶׂה
חֶסֶד לִמְשִׁיחוֹ לְדָוִד
וּלְזַרְעוֹ עַד־עוֹלָם. עֹשֶׂה
שָׁלוֹם בִּמְרוֹמָיו הוּא
יַעֲשֶׂה שָׁלוֹם עָלֵינוּ וְעַל
כָּל־יִשְׂרָאֵל, וְאִמְרוּ אָמֵן.

He brings about great victories for His king and shows kindness to His anointed one—to David and to his descendants forever. He who makes peace in His high places, may He bring about peace for us and for all Israel, and say, Amen.

19 *Y'ru es adōnoy k'dōshov ki* יִרְאוּ אֶת־יְיָ קְדֹשָׁיו כִּי
ayn machsōr liray-ov. אֵין מַחְסוֹר לִירֵאָיו.
K'firim roshu v'ro-ayvu כְּפִירִים רָשׁוּ וְרָעֵבוּ
v'dōrshay adōnoy lō yachs'ru chol וְדֹרְשֵׁי יְיָ לֹא־יַחְסְרוּ כָל־
tōv. Hōdu ladōnoy ki tōv ki טוֹב. הוֹדוּ לַיְיָ כִּי־טוֹב כִּי
l'ōlom chasdō. Pōsayach לְעוֹלָם חַסְדּוֹ. פּוֹתֵחַ
es yodecho umasbi-a l'chol אֶת־יָדֶךָ וּמַשְׂבִּיעַ לְכָל־
chai rotzōn. Boruch hagever asher חַי רָצוֹן. בָּרוּךְ הַגֶּבֶר אֲשֶׁר
yivtach badōnoy v'hoyoh adōnoy יִבְטַח בַּיְיָ וְהָיָה יְיָ
mivtachō. Na-ar hoyisi מִבְטַחוֹ. נַעַר הָיִיתִי
gam zokanti v'lō ro-isi גַּם־זָקַנְתִּי וְלֹא־רָאִיתִי
tzadik ne-ezov v'zar-ō צַדִּיק נֶעֱזָב וְזַרְעוֹ
m'vakesh lochem. Adōnoy ōz l'amō מְבַקֶּשׁ־לָחֶם. יְיָ עֹז לְעַמּוֹ
yitayn adōnoy y'voraych es amō יִתֵּן יְיָ יְבָרֵךְ אֶת־עַמּוֹ
vasholōm. בַשָּׁלוֹם.

Stand in awe of the Lord, you who are His holy ones, for there is nothing lacking to those who stand in awe of Him. Even young lions suffer want and hunger, but those who seek the Lord will not lack any good thing. Give thanks to the Lord, for He is good, for His kindness is everlasting. You open Your hand and satisfy the desire of all living. Blessed is the man who trusts in the Lord, and who makes the Lord the object of his trust. I was young and I have become old, and yet I never overlooked a deserving man who was destitute, with his children begging for bread. May the Lord give strength to His people; May the Lord bless His people with peace.

When the Blessing after the Meal is said over wine:

Boruch atoh adōnoy, בָּרוּךְ אַתָּה יְיָ,
elōhaynu melech ho-ōlom, אֱלֹהֵינוּ מֶלֶךְ הָעוֹלָם,
bōray p'ri hagofen. בּוֹרֵא פְּרִי הַגָּפֶן.

You are blessed, Lord our God, the sovereign of the world, creator of the fruit of the vine.

בְּרָכָה מֵעֵין שָׁלֹשׁ ("עַל הַמִּחְיָה")
THE BLESSING AFTER A SNACK

This blessing is said after drinking wine or after eating one of the fruits (olives, dates, grapes, figs or pomegranates) or a product, other than bread, of one of the grains (wheat, barley, spelt, oats or rye) associated with the land of Israel

Boruch atoh adōnoy,

elōhaynu melech ho-ōlom

בָּרוּךְ אַתָּה יְיָ,

אֱלֹהֵינוּ מֶלֶךְ הָעוֹלָם,

You are blessed, Lord our God, the sovereign of the world,

for grain products

al hamichyoh v'al

hakalkoloh,

עַל הַמִּחְיָה וְעַל

הַכַּלְכָּלָה,

for the sustenance and nourishment

for fruits

al ho-aytz v'al p'ri ho-aytz,

עַל הָעֵץ וְעַל פְּרִי הָעֵץ,

for the trees and their fruit,

for wine

al hagefen v'al p'ri hagefen

עַל הַגֶּפֶן וְעַל פְּרִי הַגֶּפֶן,

for the vine and its fruit,

for grain products and wine consumed together

al hamichyoh v'al

hakalkoloh v'al hagefen

v'al p'ri hagefen,

עַל הַמִּחְיָה וְעַל

הַכַּלְכָּלָה וְעַל הַגֶּפֶן

וְעַל פְּרִי הַגֶּפֶן,

for the sustenance and nourishment and the vine and its fruit

v'al t'nuvas hasodeh, v'al

eretz chemdoh tōvoh

urchovoh sherotziso v'hinchalto

la-avōsaynu le-echol mipiryoh

וְעַל תְּנוּבַת הַשָּׂדֶה, וְעַל

אֶרֶץ חֶמְדָּה טוֹבָה

וּרְחָבָה שֶׁרָצִיתָ וְהִנְחַלְתָּ

לַאֲבוֹתֵינוּ לֶאֱכֹל מִפִּרְיָהּ

v'lisbō-a mituvoh. *Rachem*	וְלִשְׂבּוֹעַ מִטּוּבָהּ. רַחֶם־
no, adōnoy elōhaynu, al	נָא, יְיָ אֱלֹהֵינוּ, עַל
yisro-ayl amecho, v'al	יִשְׂרָאֵל עַמֶּךָ, וְעַל
y'rushola-yim irecho, v'al tziyōn	יְרוּשָׁלַיִם עִירֶךָ, וְעַל צִיּוֹן
mishkan k'vōdecho, v'al	מִשְׁכַּן כְּבוֹדֶךָ, וְעַל
mizbachacho v'al haycholecho.	מִזְבַּחֲךָ וְעַל הֵיכָלֶךָ.
Uvnayh y'rushola-yim ir	וּבְנֵה יְרוּשָׁלַיִם עִיר
hakōdesh bimhayroh v'yomaynu,	הַקֹּדֶשׁ בִּמְהֵרָה בְיָמֵינוּ,
v'ha-alaynu l'sōchoh v'sam'chaynu	וְהַעֲלֵנוּ לְתוֹכָהּ וְשַׂמְּחֵנוּ
b'vinyonoh, v'nōchal mipiryoh	בְּבִנְיָנָהּ, וְנֹאכַל מִפִּרְיָהּ
v'nisba mituvoh, unvorech'cho	וְנִשְׂבַּע מִטּוּבָהּ, וּנְבָרֶכְךָ
oleho bikdushoh uvtohoroh,	עָלֶיהָ בִּקְדֻשָּׁה וּבְטָהֳרָה,

and for the produce, and for the lovely, fine and spacious land which You graciously gave to our ancestors as a heritage, to eat its fruit and to be sated with its goodness. Have mercy, Lord our God, on Israel Your people, on Jerusalem, Your city, on Zion the home of Your glory, on Your altar and on Your sanctuary. May You build up Jerusalem, the holy city, rapidly in our lifetimes. Bring us there so that we may rejoice in its rebuilding, eat of its fruit and be sated with its goodness. And there we will bless You in holiness and in purity,

on Shabbos

urtzayh v'hachalitzaynu b'yōm	וּרְצֵה וְהַחֲלִיצֵנוּ בְּיוֹם
hashabbos hazeh,	הַשַּׁבָּת הַזֶּה,

and be pleased to strengthen us on this Shabbos

on Rosh Chodesh

v'zochraynu l'tōvoh b'yōm	וְזָכְרֵנוּ לְטוֹבָה בְּיוֹם
rōsh hachōdesh hazeh,	רֹאשׁ הַחֹדֶשׁ הַזֶּה,

and be mindful of us on this holiday of the New Month

on Pesach

v'sam'chaynu b'yōm	וְשַׂמְּחֵנוּ בְּיוֹם
chag hamatzōs hazeh,	חַג הַמַּצּוֹת הַזֶּה,

v'sam'chaynu b'yōm
chag hasukkōs hazeh,

וְשַׂמְּחֵנוּ בְּיוֹם
חַג הַסֻּכּוֹת הַזֶּה,

on Shavuos

v'sam'chaynu b'yōm
chag hashovu-ōs hazeh,

וְשַׂמְּחֵנוּ בְּיוֹם
חַג הַשָּׁבֻעוֹת הַזֶּה,

on Shmini Atzeres and Simchas Torah

v'sam'chaynu b'yōm hash'mini,
chag ho-atzeres hazeh,

וְשַׂמְּחֵנוּ בַּיּוֹם הַשְּׁמִינִי,
חַג הָעֲצֶרֶת הַזֶּה,

and let us be happy on this Festival Day of Passover/Shavuos/Sukkos/ Sh'mini Atzeres,

on Rosh Hashanah

v'zochraynu l'tōvoh b'yōm
hazikorōn hazeh,

וְזָכְרֵנוּ לְטוֹבָה בְּיוֹם
הַזִּכָּרוֹן הַזֶּה,

and remember us for good on this Day of Remembrance,

ki atoh adōnoy tōv umaytiv
lakōl, v'nōdeh l'cho
al ho-oretz

כִּי אַתָּה יְיָ טוֹב וּמֵטִיב
לַכֹּל, וְנוֹדֶה לְּךָ
עַל הָאָרֶץ

for You, Lord, are good and You do good to all, and we thank You for the land

for grain products

v'al hamichyoh.
Boruch atoh adōnoy,
al ho-oretz v'al hamichyoh.

וְעַל הַמִּחְיָה.
בָּרוּךְ אַתָּה יְיָ,
עַל הָאָרֶץ וְעַל הַמִּחְיָה.

and for the sustenance. You are blessed, Lord, for the land and for the sustenance.

for fruits

v'al hapayrōs (payrōseho).
Boruch atoh adōnoy, al ho-oretz
v'al hapayrōs (payrōseho).

וְעַל הַפֵּרוֹת (פֵּרוֹתֶיהָ).
בָּרוּךְ אַתָּה יְיָ, עַל הָאָרֶץ
וְעַל הַפֵּרוֹת (פֵּרוֹתֶיהָ).

and for the fruits (its fruits). You are blessed, Lord, for the land and for the fruits (its fruits).

for wine

v'al p'ri hagofen (gafnoh).	וְעַל פְּרִי הַגֶּפֶן (גַּפְנָהּ).
Boruch atoh adōnoy, al ho-oretz	בָּרוּךְ אַתָּה יְיָ, עַל הָאָרֶץ
v'al p'ri hagofen (gafnoh).	וְעַל פְּרִי הַגֶּפֶן (גַּפְנָהּ).

and for the fruit of the vine (its vine). You are blessed, Lord, for the land and for the fruit of the vine (its vine).

for grain products and wine consumed together

v'al hamichyoh v'al p'ri	וְעַל הַמִּחְיָה וְעַל פְּרִי
hagofen (gafnoh). Boruch atoh	הַגֶּפֶן (גַּפְנָהּ). בָּרוּךְ אַתָּה
adōnoy, al ho-oretz v'al	יְיָ, עַל הָאָרֶץ וְעַל
hamichyoh v'al p'ri	הַמִּחְיָה וְעַל פְּרִי
hagofen (gafnoh).	הַגֶּפֶן (גַּפְנָהּ).

and for the sustenance and the fruit of the vine (its vine). You are blessed, Lord, for the land and the sustenance and the fruit of the vine (its vine).

(The words in parentheses are said for Israeli produce or wine.)

After food or drink not requiring either the Blessing after the Meal or the Blessing after a Snack

Boruch atoh adōnoy,	בָּרוּךְ אַתָּה יְיָ,
elōhaynu melech ho-ōlom,	אֱלֹהֵינוּ מֶלֶךְ הָעוֹלָם,
bōray n'foshōs rabōs	בּוֹרֵא נְפָשׁוֹת רַבּוֹת
v'chesrōnon, al kol mah	וְחֶסְרוֹנָן, עַל כָּל מַה
sheboroso l'hacha-yōs bohem	שֶׁבָּרָאתָ לְהַחֲיוֹת בָּהֶם
nefesh kol choy,	נֶפֶשׁ כָּל חַי,
boruch chay ho-ōlomim.	בָּרוּךְ חֵי הָעוֹלָמִים.

You are blessed, Lord our God, the sovereign of the world, creator of many kinds of life and their needs, for everything which You created to sustain all life—You are blessed, O Eternal One.

בִּרְכַּת הַמָּזוֹן לִסְעוּדַת נִשּׂוּאִין
THE BLESSING AFTER A WEDDING MEAL

Following Shir Hama-alōs (page 59), at a wedding meal, and at any meal during the next six days where the bridegroom and bride and ten or more men are present, the leader takes a cup of wine and says:

Rabōsai n'voraych. רַבּוֹתַי נְבָרֵךְ.

My friends, let us say the blessing.

The others answer

*Y'hi shaym adōnoy m'vōroch may-atoh יְהִי שֵׁם יְיָ מְבֹרָךְ מֵעַתָּה
v'ad ōlom.* וְעַד־עוֹלָם.

May the name of the Lord be blessed from now on and forever more.

The leader repeats

*Y'hi shaym adōnoy m'vōroch may-atoh יְהִי שֵׁם יְיָ מְבֹרָךְ מֵעַתָּה
v'ad ōlom.* וְעַד־עוֹלָם.

May the name of the Lord be blessed from now on and forever more.

and he continues

D'vai hosayr v'gam chorōn, דְּוַי הָסֵר וְגַם חָרוֹן,

v'oz ilaym b'shir yorōn, וְאָז אִלֵּם בְּשִׁיר יָרוֹן,

n'chaynu b'ma-g'lay tzedek, נְחֵנוּ בְּמַעְגְּלֵי צֶדֶק,

sh'ayh birkas b'nay aharōn. שְׁעֵה בִּרְכַּת בְּנֵי אַהֲרֹן.

Birshus moronon v'rabonon בִּרְשׁוּת מָרָנָן וְרַבָּנָן

v'rabōsai n'voraych וְרַבּוֹתַי נְבָרֵךְ

elōhaynu shehasimchoh אֱלֹהֵינוּ שֶׁהַשִּׂמְחָה

bim-ōnō v'she-ochalnu mishelō. בִּמְעוֹנוֹ וְשֶׁאָכַלְנוּ מִשֶּׁלּוֹ.

Sweep away sadness and anger, then even the dumb will cry out in song. Guide us in the paths of righteousness. Accept the blessing of the sons of Aaron. With the consent of all present, let us bless our God in whose presence the celebration is, and whose food we have eaten.

Boruch elōhaynu shehasimchoh
bim-ōnō v'she-ochalnu mishelō
uvtuvō cho-yinu.

בָּרוּךְ אֱלֹהֵינוּ שֶׁהַשִּׂמְחָה
בִּמְעוֹנוֹ וְשֶׁאָכַלְנוּ מִשֶּׁלּוֹ
וּבְטוּבוֹ חָיִינוּ.

Blessed is our God in whose presence the celebration is and whose food we have eaten, and through whose goodness we live.

The leader repeats

Boruch elōhaynu shehasimchoh
bim-ōnō v'she-ochalnu mishelō
uvtuvō cho-yinu.

בָּרוּךְ אֱלֹהֵינוּ שֶׁהַשִּׂמְחָה
בִּמְעוֹנוֹ וְשֶׁאָכַלְנוּ מִשֶּׁלּוֹ
וּבְטוּבוֹ חָיִינוּ.

Blessed is our God in whose presence the celebration is and whose food we have eaten, and through whose goodness we live.

All say

Boruch hu uvoruch sh'mō.

בָּרוּךְ הוּא וּבָרוּךְ שְׁמוֹ.

May He be blessed and may His name be blessed.

Continue on page 61.

At the conclusion of the Blessing after the Meal, the following blessings are said over a second cup of wine:

1. Boruch atoh adōnoy,
elōhaynu melech ho-ōlom,
shehakōl boro lichvōdo.

1. בָּרוּךְ אַתָּה יְיָ,
אֱלֹהֵינוּ מֶלֶךְ הָעוֹלָם,
שֶׁהַכֹּל בָּרָא לִכְבוֹדוֹ.

2. Boruch atoh adōnoy,
elōhaynu melech ho-ōlom,
yōtzayr ho-odom.

2. בָּרוּךְ אַתָּה יְיָ,
אֱלֹהֵינוּ מֶלֶךְ הָעוֹלָם,
יוֹצֵר הָאָדָם.

3. Boruch atoh adōnoy,
elohaynu melech ho-ōlom,

3. בָּרוּךְ אַתָּה יְיָ,
אֱלֹהֵינוּ מֶלֶךְ הָעוֹלָם,

asher yotzar es ho-odom	אֲשֶׁר יָצַר אֶת־הָאָדָם
b'tzalmō, b'tzelem d'mus	בְּצַלְמוֹ, בְּצֶלֶם דְּמוּת
tavnisō, v'hiskin lō mimenu	תַּבְנִיתוֹ, וְהִתְקִין לוֹ מִמֶּנּוּ
binyan aday ad. Boruch atoh	בִּנְיָן עֲדֵי עַד. בָּרוּךְ אַתָּה
adōnoy, yōtzayr ho-odom.	יְיָ, יוֹצֵר הָאָדָם.

4. Sōs tosis v'sogayl	4. שׂוֹשׂ תָּשִׂישׂ וְתָגֵל
ho-akoroh b'kibutz boneho	הָעֲקָרָה בְּקִבּוּץ בָּנֶיהָ
l'sōchoh b'simchoh. Boruch	לְתוֹכָהּ בְּשִׂמְחָה. בָּרוּךְ
atoh adōnoy, m'samay-ach tziyōn	אַתָּה יְיָ, מְשַׂמֵּחַ צִיּוֹן
b'voneho.	בְּבָנֶיהָ.

5. Samayach t'samach ray-im	5. שַׂמֵּחַ תְּשַׂמַּח רֵעִים
ho-ahuvim k'samaychacho y'tzir'cho	הָאֲהוּבִים כְּשַׂמֵּחֲךָ יְצִירְךָ
b'gan ayden mikedem. Boruch	בְּגַן עֵדֶן מִקֶּדֶם. בָּרוּךְ
atoh adōnoy, m'samayach choson	אַתָּה יְיָ, מְשַׂמֵּחַ חָתָן
v'chaloh.	וְכַלָּה.

6. Boruch atoh adōnoy,	6. בָּרוּךְ אַתָּה יְיָ,
elōhaynu melech ho-ōlom,	אֱלֹהֵינוּ מֶלֶךְ הָעוֹלָם,
asher boro sosōn	אֲשֶׁר בָּרָא שָׂשׂוֹן
v'simchoh, choson v'chaloh,	וְשִׂמְחָה, חָתָן וְכַלָּה,
giloh rinoh ditzoh v'chedvoh,	גִּילָה רִנָּה דִּיצָה וְחֶדְוָה,
ahavoh v'achavoh v'sholōm	אַהֲבָה וְאַחֲוָה וְשָׁלוֹם
v'rayus. M'hayroh adōnoy elōhaynu	וְרֵעוּת. מְהֵרָה יְיָ אֱלֹהֵינוּ
yishoma b'oray y'hudoh	יִשָּׁמַע בְּעָרֵי יְהוּדָה
uvchutzōs y'rushola-yim kōl	וּבְחוּצוֹת יְרוּשָׁלַיִם קוֹל
sosōn v'kōl simchoh, kōl	שָׂשׂוֹן וְקוֹל שִׂמְחָה, קוֹל
choson v'kōl kaloh, kōl	חָתָן וְקוֹל כַּלָּה, קוֹל
mitzhalōs chasonim	מִצְהֲלוֹת חֲתָנִים

maychuposom un-orim	מֵחֻפָּתָם וּנְעָרִים
mimishtayh n'ginosom.	מִמִּשְׁתֵּה נְגִינָתָם.
Boruch atoh adōnoy,	בָּרוּךְ אַתָּה יְיָ,
m'samay-ach choson im hakaloh.	מְשַׂמֵּחַ חָתָן עִם הַכַּלָּה.

1. You are blessed, Lord our God, the sovereign of the world, who created everything for His glory.

2. You are blessed, Lord our God, the sovereign of the world, the creator of man.

3. You are blessed, Lord our God, the sovereign of the world, who created man in His image, in the pattern of His own likeness, and provided for the perpetuation of his kind. You are blessed, Lord, the creator of man.

4. Let the barren city be jubilantly happy and joyful at her joyous reunion with her children. You are blessed, Lord, who makes Zion rejoice with her children.

5. Let the loving couple be very happy, just as You made Your creation happy in the garden of Eden, so long ago. You are blessed, Lord, who makes the bridegroom and the bride happy.

6. You are blessed, Lord our God, the sovereign of the world, who created joy and celebration, bridegroom and bride, rejoicing, jubilation, pleasure and delight, love and brotherhood, peace and friendship. May there soon be heard, Lord our God, in the cities of Judea and in the streets of Jerusalem, the sound of joy and the sound of celebration, the voice of a bridegroom and the voice of a bride, the happy shouting of bridegrooms from their weddings and of young men from their feasts of song. You are blessed, Lord, who makes the bridegroom and the bride rejoice together.

**The one who led the Blessing after the Meal
now takes the first cup of wine and says:**

7. Boruch atoh adōnoy,	‎7. בָּרוּךְ אַתָּה יְיָ,
elōhaynu melech ho-ōlom,	אֱלֹהֵינוּ מֶלֶךְ הָעוֹלָם,
bōray p'ri hagofen.	בּוֹרֵא פְּרִי הַגָּפֶן.

7. You are blessed, Lord our God, the sovereign of the world, creator of the fruit of the vine.

Wine from each of the two cups is poured into a third, empty cup. Then some wine from the third cup is poured back into each of the first two cups. One cup is given to the bridegroom to drink, one cup is given to the bride, and one to the leader.

בִּרְכַּת הַמָּזוֹן לִבְרִית מִילָה
THE BLESSING AFTER THE MEAL
FOLLOWING A CIRCUMCISION

Begin with Shir Hama-alōs on page 59,
then the leader continues here:

Rabōsai n'voraych.

רַבּוֹתַי נְבָרֵךְ.

My friends, let us say the blessing.

The others answer

Y'hi shaym adōnoy m'vōroch may-atoh
v'ad ōlom.

יְהִי שֵׁם יְיָ מְבֹרָךְ מֵעַתָּה
וְעַד־עוֹלָם.

May the name of the Lord be blessed from now on and forever more.

The leader repeats

Y'hi shaym adōnoy m'vōroch may-atoh
v'ad ōlom.

יְהִי שֵׁם יְיָ מְבֹרָךְ מֵעַתָּה
וְעַד־עוֹלָם.

May the name of the Lord be blessed from now on and forever more.

and he continues

Nōdeh l'shimcho b'sōch
emunoy, b'ruchim atem ladōnoy.

נוֹדֶה לְשִׁמְךָ בְּתוֹךְ
אֱמוּנַי, בְּרוּכִים אַתֶּם לַיְיָ.

We give thanks to Your name among the faithful; you are blessed by the Lord.

The others repeat

Nōdeh l'shimcho b'sōch
emunoy, b'ruchim atem ladōnoy.

נוֹדֶה לְשִׁמְךָ בְּתוֹךְ
אֱמוּנַי, בְּרוּכִים אַתֶּם לַיְיָ.

We give thanks to Your name among the faithful; you are blessed by the Lord.

Leader

Birshus ayl oyōm v'nōro,

מִשְׁגָּב לְעִתּוֹת בַּצָּרָה,

בִּרְשׁוּת אֵל אָיוֹם וְנוֹרָא,

misgov l'itōs batzoroh,

ayl ne-zor bigvuroh, adir

אֵל נֶאְזָר בִּגְבוּרָה, אַדִּיר

bamorōm adōnoy.

בַּמָּרוֹם יְיָ.

With the consent of the revered and awesome God, who is a tower of strength in times of trouble; God who is girded with power, the Lord who is mighty on high.

All say

Nōdeh l'shimcho b'sōch

נוֹדֶה לְשִׁמְךָ בְּתוֹךְ

emunoy, b'ruchim atem ladōnoy.

אֱמוּנַי, בְּרוּכִים אַתֶּם לַייָ.

We give thanks to Your name among the faithful; you are blessed by the Lord.

Leader

Birshus hatōroh

בִּרְשׁוּת הַתּוֹרָה

hak'dōshoh, t'hōroh hi

הַקְּדוֹשָׁה, טְהוֹרָה הִיא

v'gam p'rushoh, tzivoh lonu

וְגַם פְּרוּשָׁה, צִוָּה לָנוּ

mōroshoh, mōsheh eved adōnoy.

מוֹרָשָׁה, מֹשֶׁה עֶבֶד יְיָ.

With the consent of the holy, pure and clear Torah, which Moses, the Lord's servant, gave us as a heritage.

All say

Nōdeh l'shimcho b'sōch

נוֹדֶה לְשִׁמְךָ בְּתוֹךְ

emunoy, b'ruchim atem ladōnoy.

אֱמוּנַי, בְּרוּכִים אַתֶּם לַייָ.

We give thanks to Your name among the faithful; you are blessed by the Lord.

Leader

Birshus hakōhanim hal'viyim,

בִּרְשׁוּת הַכֹּהֲנִים הַלְוִיִּם,

ekro laylōhay ho-ivriyim,

אֶקְרָא לֵאלֹהֵי הָעִבְרִיִּים,

ahōdenu b'chol iyim,	אֲהוֹדֶנּוּ בְּכָל־אִיִּם,
avar'choh es adōnoy.	אֲבָרְכָה אֶת־יְיָ.

With the consent of the priests, the Levites, I will call to the God of the Hebrews. I will extol Him in all the far-flung lands; I will bless the Lord.

All say

Nōdeh l'shimcho b'sōch	נוֹדֶה לְשִׁמְךָ בְּתוֹךְ
emunoy, b'ruchim atem ladōnoy.	אֱמוּנַי, בְּרוּכִים אַתֶּם לַיְיָ.

We give thanks to Your name among the faithful; you are blessed by the Lord.

Leader

Birshus mōrai v'rabōsai,	בִּרְשׁוּת מוֹרַי וְרַבּוֹתַי,
eftach b'shir pi usfosai,	אֶפְתַּח בְּשִׁיר פִּי וּשְׂפָתַי,
v'tōmarnoh atzmōsai, boruch	וְתֹאמַרְנָה עַצְמוֹתַי, בָּרוּךְ
habo b'shaym adōnoy.	הַבָּא בְּשֵׁם יְיָ.

With the consent of all present I will open my mouth, my lips in song, and let my whole being declare: Blessed is he who comes in the name of the Lord!

All say

Nōdeh l'shimcho b'sōch	נוֹדֶה לְשִׁמְךָ בְּתוֹךְ
emunoy, b'ruchim atem ladōnoy.	אֱמוּנַי, בְּרוּכִים אַתֶּם לַיְיָ.

We give thanks to Your name among the faithful; you are blessed by the Lord.

The leader continues

Birshus moronon v'rabonon	בִּרְשׁוּת מָרָנָן וְרַבָּנָן
v'rabōsai n'voraych	וְרַבּוֹתַי נְבָרֵךְ

If there are ten men present he adds

elōhaynu אֱלֹהֵינוּ

she-ochalnu mishelō. שֶׁאָכַלְנוּ מִשֶּׁלּוֹ.

With the consent of all present, let us bless him (our God) whose food we have eaten.

The others say

Boruch (elōhaynu) she-ochalnu בָּרוּךְ (אֱלֹהֵינוּ) שֶׁאָכַלְנוּ

mishelō uvtuvō cho-yinu. מִשֶּׁלּוֹ וּבְטוּבוֹ חָיִינוּ.

Blessed is He (our God) whose food we have eaten and through whose goodness we live.

The leader repeats

Boruch (elōhaynu) she-ochalnu בָּרוּךְ (אֱלֹהֵינוּ) שֶׁאָכַלְנוּ

mishelō uvtuvō cho-yinu. מִשֶּׁלּוֹ וּבְטוּבוֹ חָיִינוּ.

All say

Boruch hu uvoruch sh'mō. בָּרוּךְ הוּא וּבָרוּךְ שְׁמוֹ.

May He be blessed and may His name be blessed.

**Continue with the Blessing After the Meal on page 61
until בעיני אלהים ואדם on page 73. Then the leader continues:**

1. Horachamon hu y'voraych 1. הָרַחֲמָן הוּא יְבָרֵךְ

avi hayeled v'imō, v'yizku אֲבִי הַיֶּלֶד וְאִמּוֹ, וְיִזְכּוּ

l'gad'lō ulchak'mō miyōm לְגַדְּלוֹ וּלְחַכְּמוֹ, מִיּוֹם

hash'mini vohol-oh yayrotzeh הַשְּׁמִינִי וָהָלְאָה יֵרָצֶה

domō vihi adōnoy elōhov imō. דָמוֹ, וִיהִי יְיָ אֱלֹהָיו עִמּוֹ.

May the Merciful One bless the child's father and mother and permit them to raise him, educate him and teach him wisdom. From this eighth day on may his blood be accepted, and may the Lord his God be with him.

2. Horachamon hu y'voraych
ba-al b'ris hamiloh, asher
sos la'asōs tzedek b'giloh,
vishalaym po-olō umaskurtō
k'fuloh, v'yit'nayhu l'ma-loh
l'mo-loh.

2. הָרַחֲמָן הוּא יְבָרֵךְ
בַּעַל בְּרִית הַמִּילָה, אֲשֶׁר
שָׂשׂ לַעֲשׂוֹת צֶדֶק בְּגִילָה,
וִישַׁלֵּם פָּעֳלוֹ וּמַשְׂכֻּרְתּוֹ
כְּפוּלָה, וְיִתְּנֵהוּ לְמַעְלָה
לְמָעְלָה.

May the Merciful One bless the *sandek* who was happy to perform this righteous act; may He reward his efforts in double measure and exalt him more and more.

3. Horachamon hu y'voraych rach
hanimōl lishmōnoh, v'yihyu
yodov v'libō b'ayl emunoh,
v'yizkeh lir-ōs p'nay
hash'chinoh, sholōsh p'omim
bashonoh.

3. הָרַחֲמָן הוּא יְבָרֵךְ רַךְ
הַנִּמּוֹל לִשְׁמוֹנָה, וְיִהְיוּ
יָדָיו וְלִבּוֹ לְאֵל אֱמוּנָה,
וְיִזְכֶּה לִרְאוֹת פְּנֵי
הַשְּׁכִינָה שָׁלֹשׁ פְּעָמִים
בַּשָּׁנָה.

May the Merciful One bless the tender eight day-old infant who was circumcised; may his hands and his heart be faithful to God. May he be worthy to appear in the divine presence three times a year.

4. Horachamon hu y'voraych
hamol b'sar ho-orloh, ufora
umotzatz d'may hamiloh, ish
hayoray v'rach halayvov avōdosō
p'suloh, im sh'losh ayleh
lō ya-aseh loh.

4. הָרַחֲמָן הוּא יְבָרֵךְ
הַמָּל בְּשַׂר הָעָרְלָה, וּפָרַע
וּמָצַץ דְּמֵי הַמִּילָה, אִישׁ
הַיָּרֵא וְרַךְ הַלֵּבָב עֲבוֹדָתוֹ
פְּסוּלָה, אִם שְׁלֹשׁ־אֵלֶּה
לֹא יַעֲשֶׂה־לָהּ.

May the Merciful One bless the *mohel* who performed the circumcision, split the membrane and drew off some blood. The efforts of a timid or faint-hearted man who did not perform these three steps would be invalid.

5. *Horachamon hu yishlach*	הָרַחֲמָן הוּא יִשְׁלַח .5
lonu m'shichō hōlaych tomim,	לָנוּ מְשִׁיחוֹ הוֹלֵךְ תָּמִים,
bizchus chasan lamulōs	בִּזְכוּת חֲתַן לַמּוּלוֹת
domim, l'vasayr b'surōs	דָּמִים, לְבַשֵּׂר בְּשׂוֹרוֹת
tōvōs v'nichumim, l'am	טוֹבוֹת וְנִחוּמִים, לְעַם
echod m'fuzor umfōrod bayn	אֶחָד מְפֻזָּר וּמְפֹרָד בֵּין
ho-amim.	הָעַמִּים.

May the Merciful One send us his faultless Messiah, in the merit of those related by circumcision, to bring good tidings and comfort to the unique people, scattered and dispersed among the nations.

6. *Horachamon hu yishlach*	הָרַחֲמָן הוּא יִשְׁלַח .6
lonu kōhayn tzedek asher lukach	לָנוּ כֹּהֵן צֶדֶק אֲשֶׁר לֻקַּח
l'aylōm, ad huchan kis-ō	לְעֵילוֹם, עַד הוּכַן כִּסְאוֹ
kashemesh v'yohalōm, va-yolet	כַּשֶּׁמֶשׁ וְיָהֲלוֹם, וַיָּלֶט
ponov b'adartō va-yiglōm,	פָּנָיו בְּאַדַּרְתּוֹ וַיִּגְלוֹם,
b'risi ho-y'soh itō hacha-yim	בְּרִיתִי הָיְתָה אִתּוֹ הַחַיִּים
v'hasholōm.	וְהַשָּׁלוֹם.

May the Merciful One send us the righteous priest who remains unseen until his shining and sparkling throne is ready; he who enveloped himself in his mantle; he who has God's covenant of life and peace.

Continue with הרחמן on page 73 or 74 to the end of the Blessing After the Meal.

סֵדֶר בְּרָכוֹת
BLESSINGS FOR ALL OCCASIONS

As a general rule, the blessing is said before doing the action or enjoying the benefit to which it refers.

בִּרְכוֹת הַנֶּהֱנִין
Blessings for the Enjoyment of Various Benefits

בָּרוּךְ אַתָּה יְיָ, אֱלֹהֵינוּ מֶלֶךְ הָעוֹלָם,

Boruch atoh adōnoy, elōhaynu melech ho-ōlom,

You are blessed, Lord our God, the sovereign of the world,

for bread

hamōtzi lechem min ho-oretz. הַמּוֹצִיא לֶחֶם מִן הָאָרֶץ.

who brings forth bread from the earth.

for cake, cookies, cereals, etc.

bōray minay m'zōnōs. בּוֹרֵא מִינֵי מְזוֹנוֹת.

creator of various kinds of foods.

for fruit that grows on trees

bōray p'ri ho-aytz. בּוֹרֵא פְּרִי הָעֵץ.

creator of the fruit of trees.

for fruits and vegetables that grow in the ground

bōray p'ri ho-adomoh. בּוֹרֵא פְּרִי הָאֲדָמָה.

creator of the fruit of the earth.

for wine

bōray p'ri hagofen. בּוֹרֵא פְּרִי הַגָּפֶן.

creator of the fruit of the vine.

for all other drinks and foods not specified above

שֶׁהַכֹּל נִהְיֶה בִּדְבָרוֹ.

shehakōl nihyeh bidvorō.

by whose word everything came into being.

for fragrant scents of spices, fruits or plants

בּוֹרֵא מִינֵי בְשָׂמִים.

bōray minay v'somim.

creator of various kinds of spices.

after using the bathroom

asher yotzar es ho-odom	אֲשֶׁר יָצַר אֶת־הָאָדָם
b'chochmoh, uvoro vō n'kovim	בְּחָכְמָה, וּבָרָא בוֹ נְקָבִים
n'kovim, chalulim chalulim.	נְקָבִים, חֲלוּלִים חֲלוּלִים.
Golui v'yodu-a lifnay chisay	גָּלוּי וְיָדוּעַ לִפְנֵי כִסֵּא
ch'vōdecho, she-im yiposayach echod	כְבוֹדֶךָ, שֶׁאִם יִפָּתֵחַ אֶחָד
mayhem ō yisosaym echod	מֵהֶם אוֹ יִסָּתֵם אֶחָד
mayhem i efshar l'hiska-yaym	מֵהֶם אִי אֶפְשָׁר לְהִתְקַיֵּם
v'la-amōd l'fonecho. Boruch	וְלַעֲמוֹד לְפָנֶיךָ. בָּרוּךְ
atoh adōnoy, rōfay chol bosor	אַתָּה יְיָ, רוֹפֵא כָל־בָּשָׂר
umafli la-asōs.	וּמַפְלִיא לַעֲשׂוֹת.

who formed man cleverly, and created in him many different organs and channels. It is clearly evident before Your glorious throne that, should one of these be wrongly opened, or one of them be wrongly blocked, it would be impossible to continue to stand before You. You are blessed, Lord, who heals all flesh in a wonderful way.

בִּרְכוֹת הַמִּצְווֹת

Blessings on the Observance of Various Commandments

בָּרוּךְ אַתָּה יְיָ, אֱלֹהֵינוּ מֶלֶךְ הָעוֹלָם,
אֲשֶׁר קִדְּשָׁנוּ בְּמִצְוֹתָיו וְצִוָּנוּ

Boruch atoh adōnoy, elōhaynu melech ho-ōlom,

asher kid'shonu b'mitzvōsov v'tzivonu

You are blessed, Lord our God, the sovereign of the world,
who made us holy with His commandments and commanded us

after washing the hands prior to eating bread

al n'tilas yodoyim.　　　　　　　עַל נְטִילַת יָדָיִם.

to wash our hands.

before putting on the arba kanfos

al mitzvas tzitzis.　　　　　　　עַל מִצְוַת צִיצִת.

to wear *tzitzis.*

before putting on a tallis

l'his-atayf batzitzis.　　　　　　לְהִתְעַטֵּף בַּצִּיצִת.

to enwrap ourselves with the *tzitzis.*

on putting up a mezuzah

likbō-a m'zuzoh.　　　　　　　לִקְבּוֹעַ מְזוּזָה.

to put up a *mezuzah.*

on immersing dishes, etc., in a mikveh

al t'vilas kaylim (keli).　　　　עַל טְבִילַת כֵּלִים (כֶּלִי).

to immerse vessels (a vessel) in a *mikveh.*

בִּרְכוֹת רְאִיָּה וּשְׁמִיעָה
Blessings of Witnessing and Experiencing

בָּרוּךְ אַתָּה יְיָ, אֱלֹהֵינוּ מֶלֶךְ הָעוֹלָם,

Boruch atoh adōnoy, elōhaynu melech ho-ōlom,

You are blessed, Lord our God, the sovereign of the world,

---

on seeing lightning and other astonishing natural phenomena

ōseh ma-asayh v'rayshis.

עֹשֶׂה מַעֲשֵׂה בְרֵאשִׁית.

who performs the work of creation.

---

on hearing thunder, or experiencing earthquakes or tornados

shekōchō ugvurosō
molay ōlom

שֶׁכֹּחוֹ וּגְבוּרָתוֹ
מָלֵא עוֹלָם.

whose power and might fill the world.

---

on seeing a rainbow

zōchayr hab'ris v'ne-emon
bivrisō v'ka-yom b'ma-amorō.

זוֹכֵר הַבְּרִית וְנֶאֱמָן
בִּבְרִיתוֹ וְקַיָּם בְּמַאֲמָרוֹ.

who remembers the covenant, fulfills His pledge and keeps His word.

---

on seeing the ocean for the first time in thirty days

she-osoh es ha-yom hagodōl.

שֶׁעָשָׂה אֶת־הַיָּם הַגָּדוֹל.

who made the great ocean.

---

on seeing trees blossom for the first time each year

shelō chisar b'ōlomō dovor
uvoro vō b'riyōs tōvōs
v'ilonōs tōvim l'hanōs
bohem b'nay odom.

שֶׁלֹּא חִסַּר בְּעוֹלָמוֹ דָּבָר
וּבָרָא בּוֹ בְּרִיּוֹת טוֹבוֹת
וְאִילָנוֹת טוֹבִים לְהַנּוֹת
בָּהֶם בְּנֵי אָדָם.

who let nothing lack from His world, but created in it beautiful creatures and lovely trees for people to enjoy.

94

shekochoh lō b'ōlomō.　　　　　　שֶׁכָּכָה לוֹ בְּעוֹלָמוֹ.

who has such phenomena in His world.

m'shaneh hab'riyōs.　　　　　　מְשַׁנֶּה הַבְּרִיּוֹת.

who varies the forms of His creatures.

shecholak maychochmosō liray-ov.　　שֶׁחָלַק מֵחׇכְמָתוֹ לִירֵאָיו.

who allots some of His wisdom to those who revere Him.

shenosan maychochmosō　　　　　שֶׁנָּתַן מֵחׇכְמָתוֹ
l'vosor vodom.　　　　　　　　לְבָשָׂר וָדָם.

who gives of His wisdom to men of flesh and blood.

shecholak mik'vōdō liray-ov.　　　שֶׁחָלַק מִכְּבוֹדוֹ לִירֵאָיו.

who allots some of His glory to those who revere Him.

shenosan mik'vōdō　　　　　　שֶׁנָּתַן מִכְּבוֹדוֹ
l'vosor vodom.　　　　　　　　לְבָשָׂר וָדָם.

who gives of His glory to men of flesh and blood.

she-osoh nisim la-avōsaynu　　　שֶׁעָשָׂה נִסִּים לַאֲבוֹתֵינוּ
bamokōm hazeh.　　　　　　　בַּמָּקוֹם הַזֶּה.

who performed miracles for our ancestors in this place.

on seeing a place where one had personally experienced a miracle

she-osoh li nays   שֶׁעָשָׂה לִי נֵס

bamokōm hazeh.   בַּמָּקוֹם הַזֶּה.

who performed a miracle for me in this place.

on hearing very good news shared by two or more people

hatōv v'hamaytiv.   הַטּוֹב וְהַמֵּטִיב.

who is good and who does good.

on hearing very bad news

dayon ho-emes.   דַּיָּן הָאֱמֶת.

the true judge.

on purchasing a new home, new furniture, clothes, etc.; on eating a fruit for the first time in the season; and on seeing a close friend after a lapse of thirty days or more

shehecheyonu v'kiy'monu v'higi-onu   שֶׁהֶחֱיָנוּ וְקִיְּמָנוּ וְהִגִּיעָנוּ

laz'man hazeh.   לַזְּמַן הַזֶּה.

who has kept us alive and sustained us and enabled us to reach this occasion.

שירי עם

Popular Songs

LIST OF SONGS

1 Ovinu malkaynu

אבינו מלכנו

Ovinu malkaynu chonaynu va-anaynu
אָבִינוּ מַלְכֵּנוּ חָנֵּנוּ וַעֲנֵנוּ

ki ayn bonu ma-asim, asayh
כִּי אֵין בָּנוּ מַעֲשִׂים, עֲשֵׂה

imonu tz'dokoh vochesed
עִמָּנוּ צְדָקָה וָחֶסֶד

v'hōshi-aynu.
וְהוֹשִׁיעֵנוּ.

Our father, our King, be good to us and answer us, even though we lack achievements. Deal with us charitably and kindly, and save us.

2 Avrohom yogayl

אברהם יגל

Avrohom yogayl
אַבְרָהָם יָגֵל,

yitzchok y'ranayn
יִצְחָק יְרַנֵּן,

ya-akōv uvonov yonuchu vō.
יַעֲקֹב וּבָנָיו יָנוּחוּ בוֹ.

Abraham rejoiced, Isaac exulted, Jacob and his children rested on it.

3 Achaynu kol bays yisro-ayl

אחינו כל־בית ישראל

Achaynu kol bays yisro-ayl,
אַחֵינוּ כָּל־בֵּית יִשְׂרָאֵל,

han'sunim b'tzoroh uvshivyoh,
הַנְּתוּנִים בְּצָרָה וּבְשִׁבְיָה,

ho-ōm'dim bayn ba-yom uvayn
הָעוֹמְדִים בֵּין בַּיָּם וּבֵין

ba-yaboshoh, hamokōm y'rachaym
בַּיַּבָּשָׁה, הַמָּקוֹם יְרַחֵם

alayhem v'yōtzi-aym mitzoroh
עֲלֵיהֶם וְיוֹצִיאֵם מִצָּרָה

lirvochoh, umay-afayloh l'ōroh,
לִרְוָחָה, וּמֵאֲפֵלָה לְאוֹרָה,

umishibud lig-uloh,
וּמִשִּׁעְבּוּד לִגְאֻלָּה,

hashto ba-agolo uvizman koriv.
הַשְׁתָּא בַּעֲגָלָא וּבִזְמַן קָרִיב.

If any of our brethren, members of the house of Israel, find themselves in trouble or in captivity, whether they are at sea or on dry land, may God take pity on them and deliver them from their trouble to well-being, from gloom to light, from captivity to freedom, now—swiftly—soon!

4 Achas sho-alti

אחת שאלתי

Achas sho-alti may-ays hashem,
אַחַת שָׁאַלְתִּי מֵאֵת ה',

ōsoh avakaysh. Shivti
אוֹתָהּ אֲבַקֵּשׁ. שִׁבְתִּי

b'vays hashem kol y'may cha-yai	בְּבֵית ה' כָּל־יְמֵי חַיַּי,
lachazōs b'nō-am hashem	לַחֲזוֹת בְּנֹעַם ה'
ulvakayr b'haycholō.	וּלְבַקֵּר בְּהֵיכָלוֹ.

There is one thing that I ask of the Lord, one thing that I desire—that I might dwell in the house of the Lord all the days of my life, witnessing the Lord's goodness and contemplating in His sanctuary.

5 Ayliyohu hanovi

אליהו הנביא

Ayliyohu hanovi,	אֵלִיָּהוּ הַנָּבִיא,
ayliyohu hatishbi,	אֵלִיָּהוּ הַתִּשְׁבִּי
ayliyohu hagil-odi.	אֵלִיָּהוּ הַגִּלְעָדִי
Bimhayroh yovō aylaynu	בִּמְהֵרָה יָבֹא אֵלֵינוּ
im moshiach ben dovid.	עִם מָשִׁיחַ בֶּן דָּוִד.

Elijah the prophet, Elijah the Tishbite, Elijah the Giladite. May he quickly come to us with the messiah, son of David.

6 Aylecha hashem ekro

אליך ה' אקרא

Aylecho hashem ekro, v'el hashem	אֵלֶיךָ ה' אֶקְרָא, וְאֶל ה'
es-chanon. Sh'ma hashem v'chonayni,	אֶתְחַנָּן. שְׁמַע ה' וְחָנֵּנִי,
hashem heyayh ōzayr li.	ה' הֱיֵה עֹזֵר לִי.

It is to You, Lord, that I call; it is the Lord to whom I appeal. Listen, O Lord, and be good to me; Lord, be my helper.

7 Im eshkochaych y'rusholo-yim

אם אשכחך ירושלים

Im eshkochaych y'rusholo-yim,	אִם אֶשְׁכָּחֵךְ יְרוּשָׁלָיִם,
tishkach y'mini.	תִּשְׁכַּח יְמִינִי.
Tidbak l'shōni l'chiki	תִּדְבַּק לְשׁוֹנִי לְחִכִּי
im lō ezk'raychi, im lō	אִם־לֹא אֶזְכְּרֵכִי, אִם־לֹא
a-aleh es y'rusholo-yim,	אַעֲלֶה אֶת־יְרוּשָׁלַיִם,
al rōsh simchosi.	עַל רֹאשׁ שִׂמְחָתִי.

If I forget you, Jerusalem, let my right hand lose its abilities. Let my tongue stick to my palate if I fail to remember you, if I fail to elevate Jerusalem above my greatest joy.

8 Omar rabbi akivo

אמר רבי עקיבא

Omar rabbi akivo,

אָמַר רַבִּי עֲקִיבָא,

zeh k'lal godōl batōroh,

זֶה כְּלָל גָּדוֹל בַּתּוֹרָה,

v'ohavto l'ray-acho komōcho.

וְאָהַבְתָּ לְרֵעֲךָ כָּמוֹךָ.

Rabbi Akiva said, "This is an important principle of the Torah: you should love your fellow as yourself."

9 Ono b'chō-ach

אנא בכח

Ono b'chō-ach g'dulas y'min'cho

אָנָּא בְּכֹחַ, גְּדֻלַּת יְמִינְךָ,

tatir tz'ruroh. Kabayl rinas

תַּתִּיר צְרוּרָה. קַבֵּל רִנַּת

am'cho, sag'vaynu taharaynu nōro.

עַמְּךָ, שַׂגְּבֵנוּ טַהֲרֵנוּ נוֹרָא.

Please, with the powerful force of Your right hand, release the captive. Accept the prayerful song of Your people; strengthen us, purify us, Awesome One!

10 Ano avdo

אנא עבדא

Ano avdo d'kudsho

אָנָא עַבְדָּא דְּקֻדְשָׁא

b'rich hu.

בְּרִיךְ הוּא.

I am a servant of the Holy One, may He be blessed.

11 Ono hashem

אנה ה׳

Ono hashem ki ani avdecho,

אָנָּה ה׳ כִּי אֲנִי עַבְדֶּךָ,

ani avd'cho ben amosecho,

אֲנִי עַבְדְּךָ בֶּן אֲמָתֶךָ,

pitachto l'mōsayroi.

פִּתַּחְתָּ לְמוֹסֵרָי.

Please, Lord, for I am Your servant. I am Your servant, the son of Your handmaid, You have loosened my bonds.

12 Ani ma-amin...b'vi-as

אני מאמין ... בביאת

Ani ma-amin be'emunoh

אֲנִי מַאֲמִין בֶּאֱמוּנָה

102

sh'laymoh b'vi-as hamoshi-ach,	שְׁלֵמָה בְּבִיאַת הַמָּשִׁיחַ,
v'af al pi sheyismahmay-ah,	וְאַף עַל פִּי שֶׁיִּתְמַהְמֵהַּ,
im kol zeh achakeh lō	עִם כָּל־זֶה אֲחַכֶּה לוֹ
b'chol yōm she-yovō.	בְּכָל־יוֹם שֶׁיָּבֹא.

I believe with perfect faith that the Messiah will come; and even though he may take his time, I will expect his arrival each and every day.

13 Ani ma-amin . . . shehabōray   אני מאמין ... שהבורא

Ani ma-amin b'emunoh	אֲנִי מַאֲמִין בֶּאֱמוּנָה
sh'laymoh shehabōray yisborach	שְׁלֵמָה שֶׁהַבּוֹרֵא יִתְבָּרַךְ
sh'mō yōday-a kol ma-asay	שְׁמוֹ יוֹדֵעַ כָּל מַעֲשֶׂה
v'nay odom v'chol machsh'vōsom,	בְּנֵי אָדָם וְכָל מַחְשְׁבוֹתָם,
shene-emar: hayōtzayr yachad libom,	שֶׁנֶּאֱמַר: הַיּוֹצֵר יַחַד לִבָּם,
hamayvin el kol ma-asayhem.	הַמֵּבִין אֶל כָּל מַעֲשֵׂיהֶם.

I believe with perfect faith that the Creator, may His name be blessed, knows all the deeds of people and all their thoughts, as it is said: "He forms their heart all together, He understands all their deeds."

14 Eso aynai   אשא עיני

Eso aynai el hehorim	אֶשָּׂא עֵינַי אֶל־הֶהָרִים,
may-ai-yin yovō ezri.	מֵאַיִן יָבֹא עֶזְרִי.
Ezri may-im hashem, ōsay shoma-yim	עֶזְרִי מֵעִם ה', עֹשֵׂה שָׁמַיִם
vo-oretz. . . . Hinayh lō yonum	וָאָרֶץ ... הִנֵּה לֹא־יָנוּם
v'lō yishon shōmer yisro-ayl.	וְלֹא־יִישָׁן, שׁוֹמֵר יִשְׂרָאֵל.

I raise my eyes to the mountains, where will help come from? Help will come to me from the Lord, creator of heaven and earth. . . . The Guardian of Israel neither sleeps nor slumbers.

15 Oshiro lashem b'cha-yai   אשירה לה' בחיי

Oshiro lashem b'cha-yai,	אָשִׁירָה לַה' בְּחַיָּי,
azam'roh laylōkai b'ōdi.	אֲזַמְּרָה לֵאלֹהַי בְּעוֹדִי.

Ye-erav olov sichi,	יֶעֱרַב עָלָיו שִׂיחִי,
onōchi esmach bashem.	אָנֹכִי אֶשְׂמַח בַּה'.
Yitamu chato-im min ho-oretz,	יִתַּמּוּ חַטָּאִים מִן הָאָרֶץ
ursho-im ōd aynom,	וּרְשָׁעִים עוֹד אֵינָם,
bor'chi nafshi es hashem,	בָּרְכִי נַפְשִׁי אֶת־ה'
hallelukoh.	הַלְלוּקָהּ.

I will sing to the Lord as long as I live, I will sing praises to my God while I exist. May my speech be pleasing to Him, as I rejoice in the Lord. May sinners disappear from the earth, and may there be no more wicked people. May my soul bless the Lord. Hallelukoh!

16 Asher boro
אשר ברא

Asher boro sosōn	אֲשֶׁר בָּרָא שָׂשׂוֹן
v'simchoh, choson v'chaloh,	וְשִׂמְחָה, חָתָן וְכַלָּה,
giloh rinoh ditzoh v'chedvoh,	גִּילָה רִנָּה דִּיצָה וְחֶדְוָה,
ahavoh v'achavoh, v'sholōm	אַהֲבָה וְאַחֲוָה, וְשָׁלוֹם
v'ray-us. M'hayroh hashem elōkaynu	וְרֵעוּת. מְהֵרָה ה' אֱלֹקֵינוּ
yishoma b'oray y'hudoh	יִשָּׁמַע בְּעָרֵי יְהוּדָה
uvchutzōs y'rusholo-yim	וּבְחוּצוֹת יְרוּשָׁלַיִם
kōl sosōn v' kōl simchoh,	קוֹל שָׂשׂוֹן וְקוֹל שִׂמְחָה,
kōl choson v'kōl kaloh.	קוֹל חָתָן וְקוֹל כַּלָּה.

Blessed is He who created joy and celebration, bridegroom and bride, rejoicing, jubilation, pleasure and delight, love and brotherhood, peace and friendship. May there soon be heard, Lord our God, in the cities of Judea and in the streets of Jerusalem, the sound of joy and the sound of celebration, the voice of a bridegroom and the voice of a bride.

17 Ashraynu
אשרינו

Ashraynu mah tōv chelkaynu	אַשְׁרֵינוּ, מַה טּוֹב חֶלְקֵנוּ,
uma no-im gōrolaynu	וּמַה נָּעִים גּוֹרָלֵנוּ,
uma yofo yerushosaynu.	וּמַה יָּפָה יְרֻשָּׁתֵנוּ.

We are fortunate: how good is our portion, how pleasant our lot and how beautiful our heritage.

18 Ato sokum   אתה תקום

Ato sokum t'rachaym
tziyōn, ki ays l'chen'noh
ki vo mō-ed.

אַתָּה תָקוּם תְּרַחֵם
צִיּוֹן, כִּי־עֵת לְחֶנְנָה
כִּי־בָא מוֹעֵד.

You will arise and have mercy on Zion, for the time will have come to be gracious to her, for the appointed time will have come.

19 Bilvovi   בלבבי

Bilvovi mishkon evneh,
lahadar k'vōdō, uvamishkon
mizbayach osim, l'karnay
hōdō. Ulnayr tomid ekach
li, es aysh ho-akaydoh,
ulkorbon akriv lō es
nafshi ha-y'chidoh.

בִּלְבָבִי מִשְׁכָּן אֶבְנֶה,
לַהֲדַר כְּבוֹדוֹ, וּבַמִּשְׁכָּן
מִזְבֵּחַ אָשִׂים, לְקַרְנֵי
הוֹדוֹ. וּלְנֵר תָּמִיד אֶקַּח
לִי, אֶת־אֵשׁ הָעֲקֵדָה,
וּלְקָרְבָּן אַקְרִיב לוֹ אֶת־
נַפְשִׁי הַיְחִידָה.

In my heart I will erect a sanctuary to glorify His honor, and in the sanctuary I will place an altar to the glories of His splendor. For the eternal light I will take the fire of the Akedah, and for a sacrifice I will offer my soul, my unique soul.

20 Boruch hagever   ברוך הגבר

Boruch hagever asher yivtach
bashem, v'hoyoh hashem mivtachō.

בָּרוּךְ הַגֶּבֶר אֲשֶׁר יִבְטַח
בַּה', וְהָיָה ה' מִבְטַחוֹ.

Blessed is the man who trusts in the Lord, and who makes the Lord the object of his trust.

21 Gam ki aylaych   גם כי אלך

Gam ki aylaych b'gay tzalmo-ves,

גַּם כִּי־אֵלֵךְ בְּגֵיא צַלְמָוֶת,

lō iro ro ki atoh	לֹא־אִירָא רָע כִּי־אַתָּה
imodi, shivt'cho umish-antecho	עִמָּדִי, שִׁבְטְךָ וּמִשְׁעַנְתֶּךָ
haymo y'nachamuni. Ta-arōch l'fonai	הֵמָּה יְנַחֲמֻנִי. תַּעֲרֹךְ לְפָנַי
shulchon neged tzor'roi, dishanto	שֻׁלְחָן נֶגֶד צֹרְרָי, דִּשַּׁנְתָּ
vashemen rōshi, kōsi revoyo.	בַשֶּׁמֶן רֹאשִׁי, כּוֹסִי רְוָיָה.
Ach tōv vochesed yird'funi	אַךְ טוֹב וָחֶסֶד יִרְדְּפוּנִי
kol y'may cha-yoi, v'shavti	כָּל־יְמֵי חַיָּי, וְשַׁבְתִּי
b'vays hashem l'ōrech yomim.	בְּבֵית־ה' לְאֹרֶךְ יָמִים.

Even though I may walk through the valley of the shadow of death, I will fear no evil for You are with me, Your rod and Your staff comfort me. You prepare a table before me in the presence of my enemies, You have anointed my head with oil, my cup overflows. May only goodness and kindness pursue me all the days of my life, and may I dwell in the house of the Lord forever.

22 Dovid melech   דוד מלך

Dovid melech yisro-ayl	דָּוִד מֶלֶךְ יִשְׂרָאֵל
chai v'ka-yom.... Simon tōv	חַי וְקַיָּם... סִמָּן טוֹב
umazol tōv y'hay	וּמַזָּל טוֹב יְהֵא
lonu ulchol yisro-ayl. Omayn.	לָנוּ וּלְכָל יִשְׂרָאֵל, אָמֵן.

David, King of Israel, lives forever. May there be a good omen and good fortune for us and for all Israel, and say Omayn.

23 Havayn yakir li   הבן יקיר לי

Havayn yakir li efra-yim, im	הֲבֵן יַקִּיר לִי אֶפְרַיִם אִם
yeled sha-ashu-im, ki miday	יֶלֶד שַׁעֲשׁוּעִים, כִּי־מִדֵּי
dab'ri bō zochor ēzk'renu ōd.	דַבְּרִי בוֹ זָכֹר אֶזְכְּרֶנּוּ עוֹד,
Al kayn homu may-ai lō rachaym	עַל־כֵּן הָמוּ מֵעַי לוֹ רַחֵם
arachamenu n'um hashem.	אֲרַחֲמֶנּוּ נְאֻם־ה'.

Is it because Ephraim is my beloved son, that he is such a lovely child, that—whenever I mention him—I yearn for him more and more? Therefore my heart longs for him; I will have pity on him, says the Lord.

24 Hu k'lal godōl

הוא כלל גדול

Hu k'lal godōl batōroh.

הוּא כְּלָל גָּדוֹל בַּתּוֹרָה.

Shivisi hashem l'negdi somid,

שִׁוִּיתִי ה' לְנֶגְדִּי תָמִיד,

hu k'lal godōl batōroh

הוּא כְּלָל גָּדוֹל בַּתּוֹרָה

uvma-alōs hatzadikim asher

וּבְמַעֲלוֹת הַצַּדִּיקִים אֲשֶׁר

hol'chim lifnay ho-elōkim.

הוֹלְכִים לִפְנֵי הָאֱלֹקִים.

This is an important principle of the Torah: I put the Lord before me at all times. This is an important principle of the Torah and among the righteous who walk before God.

25 Hōshi-oh es amecho

הושיעה את־עמך

Hōshi-oh es amecho,

הוֹשִׁיעָה אֶת־עַמֶּךָ,

uvoraych es nachalosecho, ur-aym

וּבָרֵךְ אֶת־נַחֲלָתֶךָ, וּרְעֵם

v'nas'aym ad ho-ōlom.

וְנַשְּׂאֵם עַד הָעוֹלָם.

Save Your people and bless Your possession; tend them and sustain them forever.

26 Hamal-och hagō-ayl

המלאך הגאל

Hamal-och hagō-ayl ōsi mikol

הַמַּלְאָךְ הַגֹּאֵל אֹתִי מִכָּל־

ro y'vorech es han'orim,

רָע יְבָרֵךְ אֶת־הַנְּעָרִים,

v'yikoray vohem sh'mi v'shaym

וְיִקָּרֵא בָהֶם שְׁמִי וְשֵׁם

avōsai avrohom v'yitzchok,

אֲבֹתַי אַבְרָהָם וְיִצְחָק,

v'yidgu lorōv b'kerev ho-oretz.

וְיִדְגּוּ לָרֹב בְּקֶרֶב הָאָרֶץ.

May the angel who protects me from all evil bless the youngsters, and may their reputation become like mine and that of my fathers Abraham and Isaac, and may they greatly multiply in the land.

27 Hinayh kayl y'shu-osi

הנה קל ישועתי

Hinayh kayl y'shu-osi, evtach

הִנֵּה קֵל יְשׁוּעָתִי, אֶבְטַח

v'lō efchod, ki ozi

וְלֹא אֶפְחָד, כִּי עָזִּי

v'zimros koh hashem, vaihi li

וְזִמְרָת קָהּ ה', וַיְהִי לִי

lishu-oh. Ush-avtem ma-yim	לִישׁוּעָה. וּשְׁאַבְתֶּם מַיִם
b'sosōn mima-ai-nay haishu-oh.	בְּשָׂשׂוֹן מִמַּעַיְנֵי הַיְשׁוּעָה.
Lashem haishu-oh, al am'cho	לַה' הַיְשׁוּעָה, עַל עַמְּךָ
birchosecho seloh.	בִרְכָתֶךָ סֶּלָה.

Behold, God is my salvation, I will have trust and not be afraid. Indeed, the Lord is my strength and my song and He has become my salvation. You should draw water with joy from the wells of salvation. Salvation belongs to the Lord; may Your blessing be upon Your people, Seloh.

28 Hinayh yomim bo-im   הנה ימים באים

Hinayh yomim bo-im...	הִנֵּה יָמִים בָּאִים...
V'hishlachti ro-ov bo-oretz,	וְהִשְׁלַחְתִּי רָעָב בָּאָרֶץ,
lō ro-ov lalechem v'lō	לֹא רָעָב לַלֶּחֶם וְלֹא
tzomo lama-yim, ki im	צָמָא לַמַּיִם, כִּי אִם
lishmō-a ays divray hashem.	לִשְׁמֹעַ אֵת דִּבְרֵי ה'.

Behold, days are coming when I will send a famine in the land; not a famine of bread, nor a thirst for water, but of learning the words of the Lord.

29 Hinayh mah tōv   הנה מה טוב

Hinayh mah tōv umah no-im	הִנֵּה מַה טּוֹב וּמַה נָּעִים
sheves achim gam yochad.	שֶׁבֶת אַחִים גַּם יָחַד.

How good and pleasant it is when brothers live together in harmony.

30 Uvo-u ho-ōv'dim   ובאו האבדים

Uvo-u ho-ōv'dim b'eretz	וּבָאוּ הָאֹבְדִים בְּאֶרֶץ
ashur v'hanidochim b'eretz	אַשּׁוּר וְהַנִּדָּחִים בְּאֶרֶץ
mitzro-yim v'hishtachavu lashem	מִצְרַיִם, וְהִשְׁתַּחֲווּ לַה'
b'har hakōdesh birusholo-yim.	בְּהַר הַקֹּדֶשׁ בִּירוּשָׁלָיִם.

Those who are lost in the land of Assyria and those who are exiled in the land of Egypt will come and bow down to the Lord on the holy mountain in Jerusalem.

31 V'ho-ayr aynaynu וְהָאֵר עֵינֵינוּ

V'ho-ayr aynaynu b'sōrosecho,
v'dabayk libaynu b'mitzvōsecho,
v'yachayd l'vovaynu l'ahavoh
ulyir-oh es sh'mecho, shelō
nayvōsh v'lō nikolaym v'lō
nikoshayl l'ōlom vo-ed.

וְהָאֵר עֵינֵינוּ בְּתוֹרָתֶךָ,
וְדַבֵּק לִבֵּנוּ בְּמִצְוֹתֶיךָ,
וְיַחֵד לְבָבֵנוּ לְאַהֲבָה
וּלְיִרְאָה אֶת־שְׁמֶךָ, שֶׁלֹא
נֵבוֹשׁ וְלֹא נִכָּלֵם וְלֹא
נִכָּשֵׁל לְעוֹלָם וָעֶד.

Enlighten our eyes with Your Torah, harness our hearts to Your mitzvos, and unify our resolve to love and respect Your name, so that we should never feel embarrassed or ashamed or put down.

32 Vaihi vishurun melech וַיְהִי בִישֻׁרוּן מֶלֶךְ

Vaihi vishurun melech
b'his-asayf roshay om,
yachad shivtay yisro-ayl.

וַיְהִי בִישֻׁרוּן מֶלֶךְ
בְּהִתְאַסֵּף רָאשֵׁי עָם,
יַחַד שִׁבְטֵי יִשְׂרָאֵל.

He became King of Yeshurun when the leaders of the people assembled, when the tribes of Israel were united.

33 Vahavi-ōsim וַהֲבִיאוֹתִים

Vahavi-ōsim el har kodshi,
v'simachtim b'vays t'filosi,
ōlōsayhem v'zivchayhem l'rotzōn
al mizb'chi, ki vaysi bays
t'filo yikoray l'chol ho-amim.

וַהֲבִיאוֹתִים אֶל הַר קָדְשִׁי,
וְשִׂמַּחְתִּים בְּבֵית תְּפִלָּתִי,
עוֹלֹתֵיהֶם וְזִבְחֵיהֶם לְרָצוֹן
עַל מִזְבְּחִי, כִּי בֵיתִי בֵּית
תְּפִלָּה יִקָּרֵא לְכָל הָעַמִּים.

And I will bring them to My holy mountain, and I will make them joyful in My house of prayer; their offerings and their sacrifices will find favor on My altar, for My house will be called a house of prayer for all peoples.

34 V'ya-azōr v'yogayn וִיעַזֹּר וְיָגֵן

V'ya-azōr v'yogayn v'yōshi-a
l'chōl hachōsim bō.

וִיעַזֹּר וְיָגֵן וְיוֹשִׁיעַ
לְכָל הַחוֹסִים בּוֹ.

May He help, shield and redeem all those who turn to Him for refuge.

35 V'lirushola-yim ir'cho

וְלִירוּשָׁלַיִם עִירְךָ

V'lirushola-yim ir'cho

וְלִירוּשָׁלַיִם עִירְךָ

b'rachamim toshuv, v'sishkōn

בְּרַחֲמִים תָּשׁוּב, וְתִשְׁכּוֹן

b'sōchoh ka-asher dibarto,

בְּתוֹכָהּ כַּאֲשֶׁר דִּבַּרְתָּ,

uvnay ōsoh b'korōv

וּבְנֵה אוֹתָהּ בְּקָרוֹב

b'yomaynu binyan ōlom, v'chisay

בְּיָמֵינוּ בִּנְיַן עוֹלָם, וְכִסֵּא

dovid m'hayroh l'sōchoh tochin.

דָּוִד מְהֵרָה לְתוֹכָהּ תָּכִין.

Return, out of compassion, to Your city Jerusalem, residing in it as You said You would; rebuild it soon in our time as an everlasting structure, and swiftly establish David's throne there.

36 V'atoh vonim

וְעַתָּה בָנִים

V'atoh vonim shiru lamelech,

וְעַתָּה בָנִים שִׁירוּ לַמֶּלֶךְ,

b'sif-eres m'fō-or,

בְּתִפְאֶרֶת מְפֹאָר,

v'ashray avodov hamashmi-im

וְאַשְׁרֵי עֲבָדָיו הַמַּשְׁמִיעִים

b'kōl shivchō.

בְּקוֹל שִׁבְחוֹ.

Now, children, sing to the King with glorious magnificence. Happy are His servants who raise their voices in His praise.

37 V'korayv p'zuraynu

וְקָרֵב פְּזוּרֵינוּ

V'korayv p'zuraynu mibayn hagō-yim

וְקָרֵב פְּזוּרֵינוּ מִבֵּין הַגּוֹיִם

unfutzōsaynu kanays miyark'say

וּנְפוּצוֹתֵינוּ כַּנֵּס מִיַּרְכְּתֵי

oretz. Vahavi-aynu l'tziyōn

אָרֶץ. וַהֲבִיאֵנוּ לְצִיּוֹן

ir'cho b'rinoh, v'lirushola yim

עִירְךָ בְּרִנָּה, וְלִירוּשָׁלַיִם

bays mikdosh cho b'simchas

בֵּית מִקְדָּשְׁךָ בְּשִׂמְחַת

ōlom.

עוֹלָם.

Assemble our scattered people from among the nations and gather our dispersed ones from the ends of the earth. Bring us to Zion, Your city, and to Jerusalem, Your sanctuary, in eternal joy.

38 Ur-ayh vonim

וראה בנים

Ur-ayh vonim l'vonecho,

וּרְאֵה בָנִים לְבָנֶיךָ,

sholōm al yisro-ayl.

שָׁלוֹם עַל יִשְׂרָאֵל.

May you live to see your children's children. May Israel have peace!

39 Tōv l'hōdōs

טוב להודות

Tōv l'hōdōs lashem ulzamayr

טוֹב לְהוֹדוֹת לַה׳ וּלְזַמֵּר

l'shimcho elyōn. L'hagid

לְשִׁמְךָ עֶלְיוֹן. לְהַגִּיד

babōker chasdecho ve-emunos'cho

בַּבֹּקֶר חַסְדֶּךָ וֶאֱמוּנָתְךָ

balaylōs.

בַּלֵּילוֹת.

It is good to give thanks to the Lord, to sing praises to Your name, Exalted One; to tell of Your kindness in the morning and of Your steadfastness by night.

40 Yiboneh hamikdosh

יבנה המקדש

Yiboneh hamikdosh,

יִבָּנֶה הַמִּקְדָּשׁ,

ir tziyon t'malay,

עִיר צִיּוֹן תְּמַלֵּא,

v'shom noshir shir chodosh

וְשָׁם נָשִׁיר שִׁיר חָדָשׁ

uvirnono na-aleh.

וּבִרְנָנָה נַעֲלֶה.

May the Temple be rebuilt, the city of Zion again filled. There we will sing a new song and ascend with joyous singing.

41 Yosis ola-yich

ישיש עליך

Yosis ola-yich elōko-yich

יָשִׂישׂ עָלַיִךְ אֱלֹקָיִךְ

kimsōs choson al kaloh.

כִּמְשׂוֹשׂ חָתָן עַל כַּלָּה.

May your God rejoice over you as a bridegroom rejoices over the bride.

42 Yisro-ayl b'tach

ישראל בטח

Yisro-ayl b'tach bashem,

יִשְׂרָאֵל בְּטַח בַּה׳,

ezrom umoginom hu.

עֶזְרָם וּמָגִנָּם הוּא.

Israel trusts the Lord; He is their help and protector.

43 Kōh omar hashem

כה אמר ה'

Kōh omar hashem zocharti loch

כֹּה אָמַר ה' זָכַרְתִּי לָךְ

chesed n'ura-yich ahavas

חֶסֶד נְעוּרַיִךְ אַהֲבַת

k'lulōso-yich, lechtaych acharai

כְּלוּלֹתָיִךְ, לֶכְתֵּךְ אַחֲרַי

bamidbor, b'eretz lō z'ruoh.

בַּמִּדְבָּר, בְּאֶרֶץ לֹא זְרוּעָה.

This is what the Lord said: "I remember your youthful kindness, the love of your commitment, your following Me into the wilderness, into an uncultivated land."

44 Ki l'cho

כי לך

Ki l'cho tōv l'hōdōs

כִּי לְךָ טוֹב לְהוֹדוֹת

ulshimcho no-eh l'zamayr,

וּלְשִׁמְךָ נָאֶה לְזַמֵּר,

ki may-ōlom v'ad ōlom

כִּי מֵעוֹלָם וְעַד עוֹלָם

atoh kayl.

אַתָּה קֵל.

It is good to give thanks to You and pleasant to sing praises to Your name, for You are God forever.

45 Ki mitziyōn

כי מציון

Ki mitziyōn taytzay sōroh

כִּי מִצִּיּוֹן תֵּצֵא תוֹרָה

udvar hashem mirusholo-yim.

וּדְבַר ה' מִירוּשָׁלָיִם.

Torah shall emanate from Zion and the word of the Lord from Jerusalem.

46 Kaytzad m'rak'dim

כיצד מרקדים

Kaytzad m'rak'dim lifnay

כֵּיצַד מְרַקְּדִים לִפְנֵי

hakaloh, kaloh no-oh

הַכַּלָּה, כַּלָּה נָאָה

vachasudoh,

וַחֲסוּדָה,

What does one say when dancing before a bride? "The bride is beautiful and virtuous."

47 Kol ho-ōlom

כל העולם

Kol ho-ōlom kulō gesher tzar

כָּל הָעוֹלָם כֻּלּוֹ גֶּשֶׁר צַר

m'ōd, v'ho-ikar lō l'fachayd   מְאֹד, וְהָעִיקָר לֹא לְפַחֵד
k'lol.   כְּלָל.

The whole world is a very narrow bridge, but what matters most is not to be at all afraid.

48   Lō olecho . . . She-yiboneh   לֹא עָלֶיךָ . . . שֶׁיבְנה

Lō olecho ham'lochoh   לֹא עָלֶיךָ הַמְּלָאכָה
ligmōr, v'lō atoh ven   לִגְמֹר, וְלֹא אַתָּה בֶן
chōrin l'hibotel mimenoh. . . .   חוֹרִין לְהִבָּטֵל מִמֶּנָּה . . .
She-yiboneh bays hamikdosh   שֶׁיבָּנֶה בֵּית הַמִּקְדָּשׁ
bimhayroh v'yomaynu.   בִּמְהֵרָה בְיָמֵינוּ.

Even though it may not be your responsibility to complete the job, that does not mean that you are free to disregard it. . . . May the Temple be rebuilt swiftly, in our time.

49   Layv tohōr   לב טהור

Layv tohōr b'ro li   לֵב טָהוֹר בְּרָא לִי
elōkim, v'ruach nochōn chadaysh   אֱלֹקִים, וְרוּחַ נָכוֹן חַדֵּשׁ
b'kirbi. Al tashlichayni   בְּקִרְבִּי. אַל תַּשְׁלִיכֵנִי
mil'fonecho v'ruach kodsh'cho   מִלְּפָנֶיךָ וְרוּחַ קָדְשְׁךָ
al tikach mimeni.   אַל תִּקַּח מִמֶּנִּי.

Form a pure heart for me, God, and restore the proper spirit to me. Do not reject me and do not take Your holy spirit away from me.

50   L'ma-an achai   למען אחי

L'ma-an achai v'ray-oy adab'roh   לְמַעַן אַחַי וְרֵעָי אֲדַבְּרָה
no sholōm boch. L'ma-an bays   נָא שָׁלוֹם בָּךְ. לְמַעַן בֵּית
hashem elōkaynu avakshoh   ה׳ אֱלֹקֵינוּ אֲבַקְשָׁה
tōv loch.   טוֹב לָךְ.

For the sake of my brothers and friends, let me now talk of peace. For the sake of the house of the Lord our God, let me strive after good things for you.

51   L'shonoh habo-oh

לשנה הבאה

L'shonoh habo-oh
birushola-yim hab'nuyoh.

לְשָׁנָה הַבָּאָה
בִּירוּשָׁלַיִם הַבְּנוּיָה.

Next year may we be in rebuilt Jerusalem.

52   Mah tōvu

מה טבו

Mah tōvu ōholecho ya-akōv,
mishk'nōsecho yisro-ayl. Va-ani
b'rōv chasd'cho ovō vaysecho,
eshtachaveh el haychal
kodsh'cho b'yir-osecho.

מַה טֹּבוּ אֹהָלֶיךָ יַעֲקֹב,
מִשְׁכְּנֹתֶיךָ יִשְׂרָאֵל. וַאֲנִי
בְּרֹב חַסְדְּךָ אָבֹא בֵיתֶךָ,
אֶשְׁתַּחֲוֶה אֶל הֵיכַל
קָדְשְׁךָ בְּיִרְאָתֶךָ.

How fine are your tents, Jacob, your homes, Israel. As for me, I come to Your home through Your abundant kindness; I worship in Your holy sanctuary in awe of You.

53   M'hayroh

מהרה

M'hayroh, hashem elōkaynu, yishoma
b'oray y'hudoh uvchutzōs
y'rushola-yim kōl sosōn v'kōl
simchoh, kōl choson v'kōl
kaloh, kōl mitzhalōs
chasonim maychuposom un-orim
mimishtayh n'ginosom.

מְהֵרָה, ה' אֱלֹקֵינוּ, יִשָּׁמַע
בְּעָרֵי יְהוּדָה וּבְחוּצוֹת
יְרוּשָׁלַיִם קוֹל שָׂשׂוֹן וְקוֹל
שִׂמְחָה, קוֹל חָתָן וְקוֹל
כַּלָה, קוֹל מִצְהֲלוֹת
חֲתָנִים מֵחֻפָּתָם וּנְעָרִים
מִמִּשְׁתֵּה נְגִינָתָם.

May there soon be heard, Lord our God, in the cities of Judea and in the streets of Jerusalem, the sound of joy and the sound of celebration, the voice of a bridegroom and the voice of a bride, the happy shouting of bridegrooms beneath their wedding canopies and of young men at their feasts of song.

54   Mōdeh ani l'fonecho

מודה אני לפניך

Mōdeh ani l'fonecho melech chai
v'ka-yom, shehechezarto bi

מוֹדֶה אֲנִי לְפָנֶיךָ מֶלֶךְ חַי
וְקַיָּם, שֶׁהֶחֱזַרְתָּ בִּי

| *nishmosi b'chemloh,* | נִשְׁמָתִי בְּחֶמְלָה, |
| *raboh emunosecho.* | רַבָּה אֱמוּנָתֶךָ. |

I acknowledge before You, everliving and everlasting King, that You have restored my soul to me in mercy; Your faithfulness is unbounded.

55 Mi ho-ish

מי האיש

Mi ho-ish he-chofetz cha-yim,	מִי הָאִישׁ הֶחָפֵץ חַיִּים,
ōhayv yomim lir-ōs tōv.	אֹהֵב יָמִים לִרְאוֹת טוֹב.
N'tzōr l'shōn'cho mayro,	נְצֹר לְשׁוֹנְךָ מֵרָע,
usfosecho midabayr mirmo.	וּשְׂפָתֶיךָ מִדַּבֵּר מִרְמָה.
Sur mayro va-asayh tōv,	סוּר מֵרָע וַעֲשֵׂה טוֹב,
bakesh sholōm v'rodfayhu.	בַּקֵּשׁ שָׁלוֹם וְרָדְפֵהוּ.

Who is the one who delights in life, loves days in order to see good? Guard your tongue from evil and your lips from speaking falsehood. Turn from evil and do good, seek peace and pursue it.

56 Mitzvoh g'dōloh

מצוה גדולה

| *Mitzvoh g'dōloh lihyōs* | מִצְוָה גְּדוֹלָה לִהְיוֹת |
| *b'simchoh tomid.* | בְּשִׂמְחָה תָּמִיד. |

It is a great mitzvah to be happy always.

57 Mikōlōs ma-yim rabim

מקלות מים רבים

Mikōlōs ma-yim rabim,	מִקֹּלוֹת מַיִם רַבִּים,
adirim mishb'ray yom,	אַדִּירִים מִשְׁבְּרֵי יָם,
adir bamorōm hashem.	אַדִּיר בַּמָּרוֹם ה'.

Greater than the noise of torrential waters, mightier than the waves of the sea, is the might of the Lord on high.

58 Ivdu

עבדו

| *Ivdu es hashem b'simchoh,* | עִבְדוּ אֶת־ה' בְּשִׂמְחָה, |
| *bō-u l'fonov birnonoh.* | בֹּאוּ לְפָנָיו בִּרְנָנָה. |

Serve the Lord with joy, come before Him with happy singing.

59 Ōd yishoma

Ōd yishoma b'oray y'hudoh
uvchutzōs y'rushola-yim, kōl
sosōn v'kōl simchoh,
kōl choson v'kōl kaloh.

עוד ישמע

עוֹד יִשָּׁמַע בְּעָרֵי יְהוּדָה
וּבְחוּצוֹת יְרוּשָׁלַיִם, קוֹל
שָׂשׂוֹן וְקוֹל שִׂמְחָה,
קוֹל חָתָן וְקוֹל כַּלָּה.

May there still be heard in the cities of Judea and in the streets of Jerusalem, the sound of joy and the sound of celebration, the voice of the bridegroom and the voice of the bride.

60 Am yisro-ayl chai

Am yisro-ayl chai,
ōd ovinu chai.

עם ישראל חי

עַם יִשְׂרָאֵל חַי,
עוֹד אָבִינוּ חַי.

The people of Israel lives; our Father still lives!

61 Invay hagefen

Invay hagefen b'invay hagefen
dovor no-eh umiskabel.

ענבי הגפן

עִנְבֵי הַגֶּפֶן בְּעִנְבֵי הַגֶּפֶן
דָּבָר נָאֶה וּמִתְקַבֵּל.

The mingling of grapes with other grapes is beautiful and agreeable.

62 Aytz cha-yim

Aytz cha-yim hi lamachazikim
boh v'sōm'cheho m'ushor.
D'rocheho darchay nō-am v'chol
n'sivōseho sholōm.
Hashivaynu hashem aylecho
v'neshuvoh, chadaysh yomaynu
k'kedem.

עץ חיים

עֵץ חַיִּים הִיא לַמַּחֲזִיקִים
בָּהּ וְתֹמְכֶיהָ מְאֻשָּׁר.
דְּרָכֶיהָ דַרְכֵי נֹעַם וְכָל־
נְתִבוֹתֶיהָ שָׁלוֹם.
הֲשִׁיבֵנוּ ה' אֵלֶיךָ
וְנָשׁוּבָה, חַדֵּשׁ יָמֵינוּ
כְּקֶדֶם.

It is a tree of life to those who grasp it and its supporters are happy. Its ways are pleasant and its paths are peaceful. Bring us back, Lord, to You, and we will repent; renew our days as of old.

63 Pis-chu li

Pis-chu li sha-aray tzedek,

ovō vom ōdeh koh.

Zeh hasha-ar lashem tzadikim

yovō-u vō.

פִּתְחוּ לִי

פִּתְחוּ לִי שַׁעֲרֵי צֶדֶק,
אָבֹא בָם אוֹדֶה קָה.
זֶה הַשַּׁעַר לַה' צַדִּיקִים
יָבֹאוּ בוֹ.

Open the gates of righteousness for me; I will go in and praise God. This is the gateway to the Lord through which the righteous may enter.

64 Tzavayh

Tzavayh y'shu-ōs ya-akov.

צַוֵּה

צַוֵּה יְשׁוּעוֹת יַעֲקֹב.

Give a command for the salvation of Jacob.

65 Rabōs machashovōs

Rabōs machashovōs b'lev

ish va-atzas hashem hi

sokum. Atzas hashem l'ōlom

ta-amōd, machsh'vōs libō

l'dōr vodōr.

רבות מחשבות

רַבּוֹת מַחֲשָׁבוֹת בְּלֶב
אִישׁ וַעֲצַת ה' הִיא
תָקוּם. עֲצַת ה' לְעוֹלָם
תַּעֲמֹד, מַחְשְׁבוֹת לִבּוֹ
לְדֹר וָדֹר.

Many ideas pass through a man's heart, but the Lord's plan will endure. The Lord's plan will stand firm forever; His ideas through all generations.

66 Rachaym b'chasdecho

Rachaym b'chasdecho

al am'cho tzuraynu,

al tziyōn mishkan k'vōdecho,

z'vul bays tif-artaynu.

רחם בחסדך

רַחֵם בְּחַסְדֶּךָ
עַל-עַמְּךָ צוּרֵנוּ,
עַל צִיּוֹן מִשְׁכַּן כְּבוֹדֶךָ,
זְבוּל בֵּית תִּפְאַרְתֵּנוּ.

Have mercy in Your kindness on Your nation, our Rock, and on Zion the home of Your glory, the place of our splendid Temple.

67 Rachaym no

Rachaym no hashem elōkaynu

רחם נא

רַחֵם נָא ה' אֱלֹקֵינוּ

al yisro-ayl amecho,	עַל יִשְׂרָאֵל עַמֶּךָ,
v'al yerushola-yim irecho,	וְעַל יְרוּשָׁלַיִם עִירֶךָ,
v'al tziyōn mishkan k'vōdecho,	וְעַל צִיּוֹן מִשְׁכַּן כְּבוֹדֶךָ,
v'al malchus bays dovid	וְעַל מַלְכוּת בֵּית דָּוִד
m'shichecho, v'al haba-yis	מְשִׁיחֶךָ, וְעַל הַבַּיִת
hagodōl v'hakodōsh.	הַגָּדוֹל וְהַקָּדוֹשׁ.

Have mercy, Lord our God, on Israel Your people, on Jerusalem Your city, on Zion the home of Your glory, on the kingdom of the house of David Your anointed one, and on the great and holy Temple.

68 R'tzay hashem elōkaynu רצה ה׳ אלקינו

R'tzay hashem elōkaynu b'am'cho	רְצֵה ה׳ אֱלֹקֵינוּ בְּעַמְּךָ
yisro-ayl uvisfilosom, v'hoshayv	יִשְׂרָאֵל וּבִתְפִלָּתָם, וְהָשֵׁב
es ho-avōdoh lidvir baysecho.	אֶת הָעֲבוֹדָה לִדְבִיר בֵּיתֶךָ.

Be pleased, Lord our God, with Your people Israel and with their prayer, and restore the service to Your holy Temple.

69 Rotzoh hakodōsh boruch hu רצה הקדוש ברוך הוא

Rotzoh hakodōsh boruch hu	רָצָה הַקָּדוֹשׁ בָּרוּךְ הוּא
l'zakōs es yisro-ayl, l'fichoch	לְזַכּוֹת אֶת־יִשְׂרָאֵל, לְפִיכָךְ
hirboh lohem tōroh umitzvōs,	הִרְבָּה לָהֶם תּוֹרָה וּמִצְוֹת,
she-ne-emar hashem chofetz l'ma-an	שֶׁנֶּאֱמַר ה׳ חָפֵץ לְמַעַן
tzidkō yagdil tōroh v'yadir.	צִדְקוֹ, יַגְדִּיל תּוֹרָה וְיַאְדִּיר.

The Holy One, may He be blessed, wanted to confer privileges on Israel, so He gave them Torah and mitzvos in abundance, as it is said: "The Lord wanted—because of their righteousness—to make the Torah magnificent and glorious."

70 S'u sh'orim שאו שערים

S'u sh'orim roshaychem	שְׂאוּ שְׁעָרִים רָאשֵׁיכֶם
v'hinos'u pis-chay ōlom,	וְהִנָּשְׂאוּ פִּתְחֵי עוֹלָם,
v'yovō melech hakovōd.	וְיָבוֹא מֶלֶךְ הַכָּבוֹד.

Hold up your heads, gates; raise yourselves, everlasting doors; let the King of glory enter.

71 Simchoh l'artzecho שמחה לארצך

Simchoh l'artzecho, v'sosōn
l'irecho, utzmichas keren l'dovid
avdecho, va-arichas ner l'ven yishai
m'shichecho, bimhayro v'yomaynu.

שִׂמְחָה לְאַרְצֶךָ, וְשָׂשׂוֹן
לְעִירֶךָ, וּצְמִיחַת קֶרֶן לְדָוִד
עַבְדֶּךָ, וַעֲרִיכַת נֵר לְבֶן יִשַׁי
מְשִׁיחֶךָ, בִּמְהֵרָה בְיָמֵינוּ.

Grant joy to Your land, gladness to Your city, growing strength to Your servant David, a shining light to the son of Jesse Your anointed, speedily in our days.

72 Samchaym שמחם

Samchaym b'vinyan sholaym,
b'ōr ponecho tavhikaym.

שַׂמְּחֵם בְּבִנְיַן שָׁלֵם,
בְּאוֹר פָּנֶיךָ תַּבְהִיקֵם.

Gladden them with a complete rebuilding; cause them to shine with the light of Your countenance.

73 Samchaynu שמחנו

Samchaynu hashem elōkaynu
b'ayliyohu hanovi avdecho,
uvmalchus bays dovid m'shichecho,
bimhayro yovō v'yogayl libaynu.

שַׂמְּחֵנוּ ה' אֱלֹקֵינוּ
בְּאֵלִיָּהוּ הַנָּבִיא עַבְדֶּךָ,
וּבְמַלְכוּת בֵּית דָּוִד מְשִׁיחֶךָ,
בִּמְהֵרָה יָבֹא וְיָגֵל לִבֵּנוּ.

Gladden us, Lord our God, through Elijah the prophet, Your servant, and the kingship of the house of David Your anointed—may he soon come and make us joyful.

74 Sh'ma yisro-ayl שמע ישראל

Sh'ma yisro-ayl hashem elōkaynu
hashem echod.

שְׁמַע יִשְׂרָאֵל ה' אֱלֹקֵינוּ
ה' אֶחָד.

Hear, Israel, the Lord is our God, the Lord is one.

75 Sh'ma kōlaynu

שמע קולנו

Sh'ma kōlaynu hashem elōkaynu,

שְׁמַע קוֹלֵנוּ ה' אֱלֹקֵינוּ,

chus v'rachaym olaynu, v'kabayl

חוּס וְרַחֵם עָלֵינוּ, וְקַבֵּל

b'rachamim uvrotzōn es

בְּרַחֲמִים וּבְרָצוֹן אֶת־

t'filosaynu. Hashivaynu hashem

תְּפִלָּתֵנוּ. הֲשִׁיבֵנוּ ה'

aylecho v'noshuvo,

אֵלֶיךָ וְנָשׁוּבָה,

chadaysh yomaynu k'kedem.

חַדֵּשׁ יָמֵינוּ כְּקֶדֶם.

Hear our voice, Lord our God, take pity and have mercy on us, and accept our prayer with compassion and favor. Bring us back to You, Lord, and we will return; renew our days as they used to be.

76 Shifchi chama-yim

שפכי כמים

Shifchi chama-yim libaych

שִׁפְכִי כַמַּיִם לִבֵּךְ

nōchach p'nay hashem.

נֹכַח פְּנֵי ה'.

Pour out your heart like water in the direction of the Lord's presence.

77 Tōras hashem

תורת ה'

Tōras hashem t'mimoh,

תּוֹרַת ה' תְּמִימָה,

m'shivas nofesh. Aydus hashem

מְשִׁיבַת נָפֶשׁ. עֵדוּת ה'

ne-emonoh, machkimas pesi.

נֶאֱמָנָה, מַחְכִּימַת פֶּתִי.

The Lord's Torah is perfect; it restores the soul. The Lord's testimony is reliable; it makes the simple person wise.

78 T'filoh l'oni

תפלה לעני

T'filoh l'oni chi ya-atōf,

תְּפִלָּה לְעָנִי כִי־יַעֲטֹף,

v'lifnay hashem yishpōch sichō.

וְלִפְנֵי ה' יִשְׁפֹּךְ שִׂיחוֹ.

Hashem shim-o s'filosi v'shav-osi

ה' שִׁמְעָה תְפִלָּתִי וְשַׁוְעָתִי

aylecho sovō. Al tusuyr

אֵלֶיךָ תָבוֹא. אַל־תַּסְתֵּר

ponecho mimeni b'yom tzar li.

פָּנֶיךָ מִמֶּנִּי בְּיוֹם צַר לִי.

A prayer for someone who is distressed, when he becomes faint and pours out his heart before the Lord: Lord, hear my prayer and let my cry reach You. Do not hide Your face from me in my time of trouble.